POODLE

CAROL FRISCHMANN
with DIANE MORGAN

Poodle

Editor: Matthew Haviland
Indexer: Elizabeth Walker
Designer: Angela Stanford
Series Designer: Mary Ann Kahn

TFH Publications®
President/CEO: Glen S. Axelrod
Executive Vice President: Mark E. Johnson
Publisher: Glen S. Axelrod
Associate Publisher: Stephanie Fornino

TFH Publications, Inc.®
One TFH Plaza
Third and Union Avenues
Neptune City, NJ 07753

Discovery Communications, Inc. Book Development Team: Marjorie Kaplan, President and General Manager, Animal Planet Media/Nicolas Bonard, GM & SVP, Discovery Studios Group/Robert Marick, VP, North American Licensing/Sue Perez-Jackson, Director, Licensing/Tracy Conner, Manager, Licensing

Printed and bound in China

16 17 18 19 20 21   1 3 5 7 9 8 6 4 2

Library of Congress Cataloging-in-Publication Data
Names: Frischmann, Carol, author. | Morgan, Diane, 1947- author.
Title: Poodle / Carol Frischmann with Diane Morgan.
Description: Neptune City, NJ : T.F.H. Publications, Inc., [2016] | Series:
   Animal planet. Dogs 101 | Includes bibliographical references and index.
Identifiers: LCCN 2015036491 | ISBN 9780793837366 (hardcover : alk. paper)
Subjects: LCSH: Poodles.
Classification: LCC SF429.P85 F75 2016 | DDC 636.72/8--dc23
LC record available at http://lccn.loc.gov/2015036491

This book has been published with the intent to provide accurate and authoritative information in regard to the subject matter within. While every reasonable precaution has been taken in preparation of this book, the author and publisher expressly disclaim responsibility for any errors, omissions, or adverse effects arising from the use or application of the information contained herein. The techniques and suggestions are used at the reader's discretion and are not to be considered a substitute for veterinary care. If you suspect a medical problem consult your veterinarian.

Note: In the interest of concise writing, "he" is used when referring to puppies and dogs unless the text is specifically referring to females or males. "She" is used when referring to people. However, the information contained herein is equally applicable to both sexes.

The Leader In Responsible Animal Care for Over 50 Years!®
www.tfh.com

CONTENTS

ORIGINS OF YOUR POODLE

Poodles are smart, happy companions with boundless energy and a sense of humor.

If you're considering a Poodle as your new best friend, then you're likely wondering what makes Poodles different from every other dog, why the breed was developed, and about the identity of the people and dogs of the Poodle world. In other words, you want to get to know the whole Poodle—kit and caboodle.

To understand the evolution of the Poodle, consider how close (or far) the companion dog you see down the street is from the wolf. Starting with wolves, how did people shape a breed that will jump into water and retrieve ducks for a hunter, sit in a fashionista's purse, and compete like an Olympian at a game called flyball? This change didn't happen overnight. And yes, all three varieties of Poodle—the Toy Poodle, the Miniature Poodle, and the Standard Poodle—are the same breed of dog, although some experts believe that the Toy Poodle has essentially become a separate breed. As with many ideas about Poodles, the right answer depends on which Poodle fancier you ask.

However, there are some points of agreement in Poodle lore. These memorable dogs have had a place in people's hearts for centuries. Poodles are smart, entertaining, happy companions who possess boundless energy and a sense of humor. The larger Poodles began as duck retrievers and the smaller variety as a court dog. Today, Poodles do all sorts of jobs—from truffle hunting to service work to search and rescue—and have explored many other professions you'll read about in this introduction. Despite having serious jobs to do, Poodles still have the inimitable dignity panache, and *joie de vivre* that made the French regard the *Caniche* (Poodle), of an uncertain origin, as their national dog.

THE DEVELOPMENT OF THE DOG

Like all dogs (*Canis lupus familiaris*), Poodles descend from wolves—not the gray wolf (*Canis lupus*), as was originally believed, but, according to a recent DNA study, a now-extinct ancestor from whom both species descend. The study, described in the July 2015 *Scientific American*, also found evidence of extensive gene-flow mixture from interbreeding between gray wolves and dogs. The resulting genetic similarities have made tracking the dog's genealogy misleading.

Whatever your Poodle's ancestral origin, researchers now think that about 15,000 years ago, dogs began helping humans hunt small game. Soon after this, deliberate dog burials begin to appear. The earliest dog actually on record is from a 14,000-year-old specimen discovered in Germany, lovingly buried with the remains of a man and woman. One nearly as old, and buried in similar circumstances, was found in Israel.

Earlier remains of wolf-dogs or wolves (it's still unclear which) found in Předmostí, an ancient settlement based in what's now the Czech Republic, suggest that earlier domestic canids took part in society, even ceremonies, but were treated poorly. These wolf-dogs are thought to have been confined, potentially beaten with sticks, and deliberately kept on a restricted, even poor diet, given less-favored reindeer meat rather than scavenging for leftover mammoth meat. But the verdict is still out.

Dated back to about 8,000 years ago, a site in Denmark reveals what may have been the first dog "breeds." Three distinct sizes of skeletons were found (just like today's Poodles!). The largest size apparently was used for hauling sleds, and the medium size, for hunting. The function of the smallest size remains unknown, although one could surmise that they were the first "lap dogs."

EARLY DEVELOPMENT OF THE BREED

No one is entirely sure where the Poodle originated. Judging from Mediterranean bas-reliefs, sculptures in which the primary figures are more prominent than the flat background, the Poodle may have existed as early as the first century. The Canadian Kennel Club (CKC) breed standard states that Poodles probably date back to the late Roman Empire and that the Standard Poodle was widely known in Europe by the 16th century, with the other varieties probably emerging over the next two centuries.

Research shows that dogs may share a now-extinct ancestor with gray wolves.

Poodles formally appeared in European art by the 16th century. One famous example of what might be a Poodle, according to the Metropolitan Museum of Art's *A Handbook to the Loan Exhibition of French Tapestries: Mediaeval, Renaissance, and Modern*, can be found in the final scene of the world-famous *Lady and the Unicorn* tapestry series, woven in 16th-century Flanders. Thereafter, both small and large Poodles featured in art are increasingly common. From the late 1700s on, Poodles of all three varieties—Standard, Miniature, and Toy—are mentioned or pictured.

BREED HISTORY IN GERMANY AND FRANCE

While some say Poodles date back to the Roman Empire, many say they were developed more recently in Germany. The name Poodle comes from the German *pudeln*, meaning "to splash in water." This term was chosen because the Standard variety was popular with German waterfowl hunters for retrieving downed ducks from water. Those retrieving dogs, also called *Canis familiaris aquaticus*, wore a unique clip to help them move through the water while keeping sensitive joints and organs covered with fur.

In France, the Standard Poodle worked as both a duck dog and truffle hunter. The Miniature and Toy varieties worked in entertainment and as companion dogs in the French court. The French court circles and the Poodle's battlefield history earned him the popular but incorrect title "French Poodle." Standard Poodles also worked pulling milk carts and as rabbit-hunting dogs.

BREED HISTORY IN THE UNITED STATES

Poodles have been part of dog life in the United States and Canada since the late 19th century. The breed became wildly popular, however, between 1949 and 1969, which was the year that Poodle Vicky (Nixon) made it to the White House as a member of America's First Family. One-third of all new American Kennel Club (AKC) registrations that year were for Poodles. The club hired a full-time staff person to handle the glut of Poodle paperwork. Poodles went on to have one of the longest-running streaks ever as America's most popular breed, taking the number-one spot in AKC breed registrations from 1960 through 1982. Nor was the craze limited to the dog himself. Poodle skirts, usually white or pink and featuring the silhouette of a Poodle, became a fad.

Well into the 21st century, the Poodle has remained one of the most popular breeds. This adaptable breed does many jobs well. Modern poodles compete in conformation, obedience, rally, and other sports competitions. They serve as therapy dogs, assistance dogs, and family companions. In addition, they still compete in field trials and work as duck-retrieving dogs.

RECOGNITION OF BREED BY MAJOR CLUBS

All major kennel clubs recognize the Poodle, including the AKC, CKC, United Kennel Club (UKC), UK-based Kennel Club (KC), and Belgium-based Fédération Cynologique Internationale (FCI), also known as the World Canine Organization. Most clubs differentiate between the Standard, Miniature, and Toy varieties.

Beyond the officials of major kennel clubs, many people have played important roles in Poodle history. The following are just some of the exceptional people who have influenced the development of the Poodle over the last few hundred years.

• Leading Poodle breeder Arlene Erlanger, owner of Pillicoc Kennels, initiated a campaign in January 1942 to recruit dogs for military service during World War II. This movement birthed a nationwide program known as Dogs for Defense, which gathered dogs for the United States military. Standard Poodles never served on the front lines but did guard military buildings in America. Poodles were eventually removed from the list of eligible breeds.

• Jean Lyle of Canada started the Wycliffe Kennel in the 1950s. Her kennel bred more than 1,000 Standard Poodles, hundreds of whom became champions. Lyle gave each dog in many of Wycliffe's litters names starting with the same letter

The Standard Poodle was popular with German waterfowl hunters for retrieving downed ducks from water.

(one litter had Thomas, Timothy, Theresa, etc.) and purportedly completed the alphabet almost half a dozen times, give or take a few letters. Many Standard Poodles alive today are descendents of Wycliffe Kennel offspring.

- Rebecca Mason of Bel Tor Poodles became the president of the Poodle Club of America (PCA) in the early 1970s. Mason created what has since become the PCA Regional Specialty and blocked the club from banning corded Poodles in competition. She has been considered the top breeder of American Poodle champions in history.
- Lynn Brucker (with help from her husband, Roger) began the Standard Poodle Database. Frustrated with her physical stud books, which were laborious to search through and only covered champion dogs, Brucker started collecting stud books from breed clubs around the world and compiling Standard Poodle records on her laptop in the early 1990s. By 2014, the Standard Poodle Database included over 211,000 Standard Poodles, providing pedigrees, offspring lists, coefficients of inbreeding, and more.

MEMORABLE POODLES

Some Poodles are memorable because they were instrumental in establishing what we think of when someone says "Poodle." Some we remember because of their show history or athletic prowess. Other Poodles are legends because of their people. Finally, some are unforgettable because of their revolutionary accomplishments.

- In 1890, Ch. Achilles became the first Poodle to win the Champion title in England. Ch. Achilles was corded, no less. His cords were said to be 30 inches (76 cm) long!
- The legendary Ch. Nunsoe Duc de la Terrace of Blakeen, who in 1935 became the first Poodle to win Best in Show at the Westminster Kennel Club Dog Show, is behind the breeding of most of today's Standard Poodles.
- Am. Eng. Can. Ch. Bibelot's Tall Dark and Handsome CDX, owned by Susan Fraser, had 31 Bests in Show when he retired in 1968.
- The first CKC Working Certificate for a Poodle, awarded for a hunting test, was earned on June 29, 1986, by Tudorose Madame Katy CDX WC.
- Starting in 1988, John Suter drove the first Iditarod teams featuring Standard Poodles to race about 1,000 miles (1,609.5 km) through Alaska. Suter's teams, which also featured Siberian Huskies, accomplished this feat multiple times, but his Poodles weren't able to withstand the Alaskan cold as well as other breeds were. Now the restrictions on competing dogs are more stringent.
- The first AKC Junior Hunter (JH) title won by a Standard Poodle was earned in 1998 by Am. Can. Ch. Oakwind's Time to Burn, who would win more than 20 titles overall!

To learn more about Poodles and their people, you can read about them, and you should. In addition, meet as many Poodles and Poodle people as you can. You're considering a lifetime together, so take your time.

The Poodle has been a popular breed for many years.

CHARACTERISTICS OF YOUR POODLE

A Poodle of any variety is the companion of a lifetime for a person who enjoys keeping up with a dog possessing energy and intellect. Although developmentally Poodles are puppies only until they are a year old, most owners say that they play like puppies for most of their lives.

A POODLE OVERVIEW

The Poodle is one of the most popular dog breeds in America, and that popularity extends worldwide. Highly intelligent and adaptable, Poodles charm almost everyone with their remarkable sense of humor and sweet disposition. Available in many colors and three recognized varieties, they are faithful, devoted companions to their families.

Of the three breed varieties, the smallest Poodle, the Toy, is popular with apartment owners, older people, and those who enjoy traveling with a small pet. The Miniature Poodle is small enough to suit apartment living and large enough to be a child's companion. The Standard Poodle, originally a water retriever, enjoys life as a versatile companion who can work in therapy, hunting, or sports.

Traits that make the Poodle especially popular include the fact that he gets along well with his people; that his shed hair is removed through grooming rather than sticking to the furniture or falling out willy-nilly; and that he's available in so many color-and-size combinations.

Points that you should be aware of include the following:

• All three Poodle varieties require grooming on a regular basis. Pet Poodles need a major clipping every four to six weeks. Their faces (and sometimes other points) require periodic trims between major clippings. A show Poodle needs grooming every day and continuous trimming and clipping to maintain his show coat.

Dog Tale

A reporter asked the late Anne Rogers Clark, the first woman to win Best in Show at the famous Westminster Kennel Club Dog Show, "Why are you passionate about Poodles?" She replied, "They're Labradors with a college education. After a day of retrieving, your Lab wants to curl up and snore in front of the fire. A Poodle wants to be a fourth at bridge and tell naughty stories." Of all the stories I've heard about Poodles, this one describes them best.

- Poodles do not like to be left alone for long periods. If your Poodle would be home alone all day every day, maybe this isn't the breed for you. Look further to find a breed that is less dependent on its people.
- Many people assume that because of their small size, Toy Poodles are ideal for families with small children. This is a mistaken impression. Small children still working on their coordination and balance (or those looking for a hardy companion) will be too rough for this delicate size variety. A Miniature Poodle is a more appropriate companion.

PHYSICAL CHARACTERISTICS

The image most people have of the Poodle comes either from a cartoon or from a television-broadcast dog show—an exaggerated creature, with petite legs and hind end, and a Lady Gaga hairdo. That picture is true enough for those Poodles who live as show dogs for a few years of their lives. However, this is not what most Poodles look like. After all, you can make hair do just about anything.

Originally retrieving water dogs, Poodles reflect the purpose for which they were bred. Without all that hair, you can see that they look capable of working, with a body that is square, well proportioned, and athletic. True to their nature as running, jumping, and playful dogs, Poodles cover ground effortlessly, head and tail up.

The Poodle, except in his extreme-makeover looks, is dignified. In his show clips (haircuts), he is unmistakable for any other breed. In his sporting or pet clips, you will still recognize him. He has been called the tourist of dogs, always watching what's around him. Because the Miniature and Toy varieties originated from the Standard, the two smaller varieties exhibit the same active intelligence and grace.

BREED STANDARD

Each purebred-dog registry has a breed standard that describes that registry's ideal Poodle. The breed standard explains which physical attributes and character traits are acceptable for show competition under its rules. The American Kennel Club (AKC) is the predominant registry in the United States. Canada has the Canadian Kennel Club (CKC). The largest international group, the Fédération Cynologique Internationale (FCI), also known as the World Canine Organization, has its headquarters in Belgium.

Each club's standards and rules are slightly different. The AKC breed standard specifies that Standard Poodles should be more than 15 inches (38 cm) tall, Miniature Poodles should be more than 10 inches (25.5 cm) tall but fewer than

15 inches (38 cm), and Toy Poodles should be 10 inches (25.5 cm) or shorter. In contrast, the FCI recognizes four sizes of Poodles (who are called *Caniches* in French): Standard, Medium, Miniature, and Toy.

Despite these various designations, the AKC considers the Poodle one breed governed by one breed standard, only varying by size. However, the three size varieties are classified under two AKC breed groups. Standard Poodles and Miniature Poodles are members of the Non-Sporting Group, while Toy Poodles belong to the Toy Group.

Incidentally, invented names for Poodle sizes, such as "teacup," "imperial," and "king," are marketing gimmicks without meaning among knowledgeable Poodle people. The use of these terms is usually a sign that the breeder is out of the mainstream and may represent a puppy mill. If you are determined to work with such a breeder, be excessively careful about health certifications.

BODY DESCRIPTION

The AKC breed standard for Poodles provides great detail about how a Poodle should look. Refer to the standard for the particulars, but generally, Poodles should appear squarely built with a strong appearance. What breeders call the "topline" (the area from the shoulders to the base of the tail) should be level. The chest should be deep, and the height at the shoulders should about equal the length of the body. The Standard Poodle is a dog who works. The two smaller varieties are smaller versions of the same body type.

The breed standard also calls for tail docking, but this controversial practice of removing part of a dog's tail has been banned or restricted in many countries. Its cosmetic use is opposed by many, including the American Veterinary Medical Association (AVMA), which supports the removal of ear cropping (removing part of each ear) and tail docking from breed standards.

COAT

The adult Poodle's coat is dense, has a harsh texture, and can be worn curly or corded. Growing continuously until trimmed, the curly coat is maintained by clipping every four to six weeks and periodically brushing so that mats and felting do not occur. Most pet and show people clip and comb through their Poodle's coat.

When a Poodle's coat is left untrimmed and uncombed, the continuously growing hair can be coiled into cords. Corded coats hang in tight ropes that look like dreadlocks. Seldom seen, they are more difficult to maintain than curly coats. Drying a corded coat can take several days.

When a Poodle's coat is left untrimmed and uncombed, the hair can be coiled into cords.

Clips

Almost any Poodle, other than those who have been completely corded, has been clipped and groomed. Clipping and grooming completely change the appearance of the coat. The clip you select is also a major determining factor for either the work or the expense of maintaining your dog.

Clips for show Poodles require more maintenance than those for companion or working Poodles. Moreover, only certain clips are acceptable for conformation. While show Poodles younger than a year old can wear the Puppy clip, older Poodles are restricted to two others: the English Saddle and the Continental clip. Corded coats are also acceptable. The Sporting clip is allowed only in the Stud Dog and Brood Bitch classes and in noncompetitive Parade of Champions events. (These clips are described in more detail in Chapter 5.)

For companion Poodles, pet clips, like the sporting and the lamb trim, are practical and require less grooming than any of the regular show clips. In fact, some owners who keep their Poodles short coated will admit to not brushing them very often between grooming sessions. Remember, the more hair your Poodle has, the more grooming is required.

The clip is a major determining factor for either the work or the expense of maintaining a Poodle.

COLORS

The AKC breed standard calls for a solid coat color. Multicolored (or "parti-colored") Poodles are not show eligible. Coat colors include black, blue, gray, silver, brown, beige, café au lait, apricot, cream, and white. Sometimes ear feathering and ruff tips are a different shade of the coat color.

The breed standard is specific about the color of nose, lips, eye rims, and toenails. Certain coat colors require certain colors for these features, so while a brown Poodle with a liver-colored nose and dark amber eyes is acceptable for conformation, a blue Poodle should have a black nose and "very dark" eyes.

Some people believe that temperament varies with coat color. Most experts say that there is no linkage between genes for temperament and color and that that myth came from dogs within certain genetic lines who all tended to have the same color and temperament. What people who love Poodles say is that no matter what color they are, they are beautiful.

BREED CHARACTER

Well-bred Poodles are hardy, steady, calm, and easily trainable. They are characters, with a sweetness and kindness their families love. People-oriented dogs, they want to be around you, no matter where you are. They'll follow you through the house watching what you're doing, looking for opportunities to participate. If you're working in the yard, they'll be with you, especially if there's any possibility you'll respond to the ball they've dropped at your feet.

Some Poodles are birdy, while others don't go anywhere without something in their mouth. Some run and jump for the fun of it. Some are unflappable. Some are performers who will do anything you ask so long as someone is watching and applauding. These personality traits are what distinguish the great retrievers from the great obedience dogs, the rally and freestyle dogs from the therapy dogs. Versatile and with some temperament variation, Poodles have one thing that doesn't change—their love of people.

Poodles are also highly intelligent, which is a blessing and a curse. Yes, they are easily trainable. They can be obedience and trick superstars. However, they also learn quickly how to manipulate an unsuspecting owner. Accordingly, you'll want to keep your keenly interested Poodle's mind busy with activities such as obedience training, a hunt test, or an afternoon of fun backyard games.

One reason people love Poodles is because they are comic. Imbued with a wonderful sense of humor, these dogs love games of all kinds. (In fact, they are happy to make anything a game!) They are also sensitive, and being excluded from activities hurts them. You may know this Poodle: he pulls tissues from the box and toilet paper from the roll because it makes his owner get up and pay attention to him. Because you are proactive, you would keep him busy and exclude him from areas where these toiletries are available until he's retrained. Poodle people will laugh and tell you that the best-trained Poodles will still pull tissues and toilet paper out for fun, as if they can't help themselves.

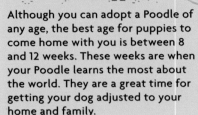

PUPPY POINTER

Although you can adopt a Poodle of any age, the best age for puppies to come home with you is between 8 and 12 weeks. These weeks are when your Poodle learns the most about the world. They are a great time for getting your dog adjusted to your home and family.

Poodles seem to understand when their humans don't feel well. Such Poodles lie next to their owners until their natural exuberance overtakes them and they poke their long, bony noses into them. "Wouldn't you feel better if you took me for a walk?" their expressions seem to say. A Poodle might also bring you the leash or a toy that he offers to share with you. And as every Poodle person will tell you, these dogs will also put their mouth around your wrist—not in a bite, because there's no pressure, but as if they are saying, "I'm here."

LIVING WITH A POODLE

An excellent and energetic companion dog, the Poodle wants to be a complete member of the family—to go where you go and do what you do. Poodles are, after all, the tourists of dogs. They enjoy learning new things and are cooperative when they see the sense in cooperation. They make noise when a stranger approaches, but they are not true guard dogs. When you go for errands, they want to join you, and while you're driving, they want you to talk to them.

Poodles sometimes seem to read your thoughts. If you plan to do some cooking, they will meet you in the kitchen. If you plan to bathe them, they'll disappear. After a day of romping in the backyard or working as your hunting dog, they may curl up with the family and watch television—or they may be ready for night maneuvers with the neighborhood kids.

If you are away at work all day, make accommodations for your Poodle. He needs and wants companionship and attention. The thoughtful owner gets up early and walks her dog and takes him out again immediately upon returning home. In the interim, Poodles need something to occupy them—either toys to make them think or companionship through dog daycare or a noontime dog walker. If this is not possible, then depending on his age, yours may not be content and may perform naughty deeds to suggest that more attention is better. Poodles need activity, both physical and mental, every day, along with the companionship of their people.

ENVIRONMENT

Despite their (peculiar) AKC classification as either non-sporting or toy dogs, Poodles were bred from retrieving dogs. Athletic companions with great stamina, they enjoy having somewhere to play, run, and explore. Standards and Miniatures are well suited to the country or to homes with backyards. Although apartment dwellers can consider the Toy Poodle (who requires less space), depending on the individual Toy, his requirement for exercise may be significant.

EXERCISE

Poodles need ample exercise, which makes them great candidates for sports— organized or simply between you and them—and for adventures. Skijoring, rally obedience, flyball, flying disc, jogging, and field trials are all events in which

All young and adult Poodles need to run and play every day.

Poodles excel. Standard and Miniature Poodles do best when their owners provide a fenced-in area in which they can exercise while being supervised. Whatever your setup, frequent walks and energetic play are required to meet your Poodle's needs.

Know that Standards and Minis are among those dogs who cause trainers to say, "A tired dog is a good dog." If you're looking for a couch potato or a dog who requires little to moderate exercise, look to another breed or an elder Poodle. All young and adult Poodles need to run and play every day.

SOCIABILITY
Highly social, Poodles want to be spoken to and admired by everyone. Most Poodles appreciate petting from a friendly stranger on the street. In fact, when they go for walks, some Poodles seem to seek out attention.

With Children
Poodles accustomed to children enjoy their games and can be excellent companions. Most Poodles tolerate being dressed in Halloween costumes and paraded as the star of a backyard circus. Because they easily learn games and tricks, Poodles can create a rewarding experience for kids learning to train their dog. Most breeders caution that Toy Poodles are too delicate for children's roughhousing, but Miniatures and Standards usually make excellent friends for afternoon adventures.

With Strangers
Generally, Poodles are not savvy guard dogs. They do not have the instincts to patrol your property or the looks to intimidate strangers. However, there are stories (for example, John Steinbeck's Poodle barking at bears in *Travels With Charley: In Search of America*) in which an individual Poodle displays great heroism in protecting his family. Your Poodle will probably bark at a stranger at your door, but as long as he is well socialized, he will accept strangers when introduced by you. If you are looking for protection, another dog might be a better fit.

With Other Dogs and Pets
Poodles usually love their fellow pets if they have been raised with other dogs and cats. If you want your Poodle to know that cat chasing is a no-no and that other dogs and cats are his best friends, then fill his life between the ages of 8 and 12 weeks with friendly dogs and cats.

Poodles usually love their fellow pets if they have been raised with other dogs and cats.

Poodles usually love their fellow pets if they have been raised with other dogs and cats.

GROOMING NEEDS

When you commit to a companion Poodle, you must decide whether to groom and clip him yourself or budget for your new best human friend—your groomer— to provide regular clipping and grooming. Most people can readily learn to groom their own dogs. Alternatively, professional groomers are happy to provide this service. Clipping every four to six weeks is a requirement for the lifetime of your companion. Otherwise, his coat will become matted and unsightly as well as unhealthy.

HEALTH ISSUES

Like all popular dog breeds, Poodles suffer from signature health issues. While well-bred Poodles are generally healthy because of the care breeders take in screening prospective parents and new puppies for genetic diseases, you must be careful in your choice of Poodle. Considering common inherited issues before adoption is critical to avoiding heartbreaking health problems.

Good breeders will want to discuss with you the screening they've done on the parents of the litter as well as the individual puppies. Genetic tests are not available for all the serious health problems that can arise, but a combination of the available tests and a veterinary examination done by a clinician familiar with Poodle health issues can help you avoid the most common foreseeable problems. See Chapter 6 for information on common genetic health issues in Poodles.

THE MYTH OF THE HYPOALLERGENIC DOG

Some books and articles claim that Poodles are hypoallergenic dogs. The online Merriam-Webster dictionary defines "hypoallergenic" as "having little likelihood of causing an allergic response." In fact, neither the Poodle nor any other dog breed is hypoallergenic. As has been known for many years but not well understood, it's not a dog's coat that provokes allergies but proteins in his saliva. Then the dog's own grooming process, licking his hair, distributes the saliva onto his coat as well as into the air.

However, it is true that many allergy sufferers can tolerate Poodles better than other dogs. Here's the reason why. Rather than simply falling out, as it does in many breeds, loose hair collects in mats within the Poodle's coat. He typically carries this hair with him until the next time he's brushed or taken to the groomer. Poodles are not hypoallergenic, as an allergy sufferer who tried to groom one would find. However, if you've got to have a dog and you're allergic, you might spend a few days with a friend's Poodle and see what your experience is.

TRAINABILITY

Poodles are so intelligent that most people find themselves being trained by them. Able to learn to participate in any canine sport and to work as search-and-rescue dogs, health aids, or cart or sled dogs, Poodles are not only trainable but also adaptable in what they can learn to do.

However, personality does make a difference. In addition to his intelligence and his willingness to work and learn, your Poodle's temperament determines whether he will be successful at your chosen field for him. Finding a Poodle who has the breeding to do what you want is an important component of whether your dog will be trainable for your purpose.

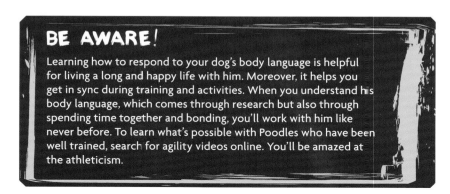

BE AWARE!

Learning how to respond to your dog's body language is helpful for living a long and happy life with him. Moreover, it helps you get in sync during training and activities. When you understand his body language, which comes through research but also through spending time together and bonding, you'll work with him like never before. To learn what's possible with Poodles who have been well trained, search for agility videos online. You'll be amazed at the athleticism.

Some aspects of performance are not trainable but are governed by innate drives. In other words, the related characteristics come from the genes, the breeding. That's one reason why you'll see kennels that specialize in hunting dogs turning out more hunting dogs and kennels that produce excellent obedience dogs whelping more excellent obedience dogs. The drives for hunting and retrieving, for unflappability and the love of the water, for persistence, are innate characteristics that an individual puppy has at birth.

Training does wonders, but it doesn't create the drive or quality of personality that is embodied in a gifted performer. Temperament testing is one way breeders can compare puppies within a litter to determine the best match for each owner. Trainers and breeders have different forms of the test, depending on their special circumstances. Such tests, conducted at 49 days of age or thereabouts, are done by people unfamiliar to the puppies and given in an unfamiliar place.

The evaluator tests the puppies to gauge attraction to people, amount of struggle against restraint, sensitivity to noise and touch, terrain courage, food motivation, persistence, and energy level. Sometimes special attributes, such as retrieval skills or bird attraction, are included. From these tests, the breeder matches puppies to their prospective homes, based on the plans the family has for their puppy. Based on these tests, breeders can also advise families of the types of behavior that will be more challenging for their individual puppy.

For the many things training can accomplish, it doesn't change the fundamental character of the breed or the temperament of the dog. Poodles are active dogs, adaptable to many different sorts of activities. Choose a healthy Poodle from a reputable breeder. A healthy Poodle of any variety can be an athlete, a therapy dog, a companion. Equally important, no matter what variety he is, your Poodle will need periodic grooming and a lot of exercise and face time with you every day. A good-fit Poodle owner is excited to spend several hours every day with her dog, exercising, grooming, and hanging out together.

SUPPLIES FOR
YOUR POODLE

Before your Poodle comes home, the most important thing you can do is to educate yourself about what he needs to be safe and happy. Every dog needs a place to sleep, food to eat, and accessories for safety and fun. Gather the following supplies before you bring your canine companion home, or put them on your shopping list if you already have him.

BEDS

While your Poodle may use his crate as a bed during crate training and housetraining, you should buy him his own bed when he's ready to make his own bedtime decisions. A dog bed can allow for decorative properties, depending on the aesthetic you're going for, but choose comfort over looks, because your Poodle is going to spend more time on it than you will admiring it.

Some dog beds offer orthopedic support, which can be helpful for dogs with arthritis. Others are poufy enough for your buddy to sink into. Some dog beds have walls and sides to offer the sense of enclosure. You can even get memory foam, if your dog leaves his impression in yours! Senior dogs may need a leak-proof bed liner if they have trouble with incontinence.

As for placement, find a place where he can lie comfortably and observe what's going on while staying warm, rested, and out of the commotion. This last part will come in handy when your Poodle is ready to snooze while you're still up playing cards. If you buy your dog a bed and find that he ends up sleeping somewhere else, note the attributes of his preferred sleeping spot. Then either move his bed there or get him a bed that feels more like the material he prefers.

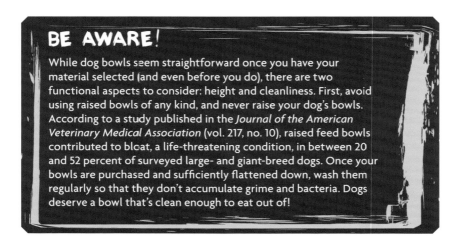

BE AWARE!

While dog bowls seem straightforward once you have your material selected (and even before you do), there are two functional aspects to consider: height and cleanliness. First, avoid using raised bowls of any kind, and never raise your dog's bowls. According to a study published in the *Journal of the American Veterinary Medical Association* (vol. 217, no. 10), raised feed bowls contributed to bloat, a life-threatening condition, in between 20 and 52 percent of surveyed large- and giant-breed dogs. Once your bowls are purchased and sufficiently flattened down, wash them regularly so that they don't accumulate grime and bacteria. Dogs deserve a bowl that's clean enough to eat out of!

Use an adjustable collar that's extra tough and has good hardware.

BOWLS

Food and water are what your Poodle needs to survive. Without anything else in this chapter, your dog would need these two things. Despite the dog bowl's ordinary nature, this tool is an essential part of that equation. Luckily, you don't have to look far to find the best bowls for your dog. Your Poodle should have weighted, dishwasher-safe stainless-steel bowls for his food and water. While these may not be the most exciting choices, they are the safest and most practical for several reasons.

Beyond being easier to clean and heavy enough to reduce spilling, stainless-steel bowls avoid the hazards of those made from other materials. Many plastic bowls, for example, contain BPA and other hazardous chemicals, and ceramic and stoneware dog bowls are often covered with toxic glaze or paint, all of which may contaminate food and water. These materials are also prone to cracks and crevices, which foster bacterial growth. Stainless-steel bowls won't contaminate their contents and are unlikely to amass bacteria when regularly washed.

The strength of the material is another important factor. Plastic bowls are prone to being chewed by dogs who feel nervous, overstimulated, or just ready for something to chew. Meanwhile, glass and ceramic bowls break easily when

dropped. Stainless-steel bowls don't attract chewing and should last your
Poodle's entire life with proper care.

COLLARS

Use flat nylon adjustable buckle collars that are extra tough and have good
hardware. Toy Poodles need extra-small collars (6–11 inches [15–28 cm]). Miniature
Poodles generally use small collars (10–15 inches [25–38 cm]). Standard Poodles
need larger collars (15–24 inches [38–61 cm]). It's a good idea to purchase two;
late one night, your Poodle will somehow get his collar off and chew through it.
Don't use a choke collar on your Poodle, because it can injure his throat.

CRATES

Crates are helpful when you're housetraining and come in handy throughout
your Poodle's life. They are not prisons for your dog (and should be used
appropriately sparingly) but more like the den that his wolf ancestors didn't feel
quite right without. And better than the wolves had it, your dog will have his
crate all to himself!

   You should keep one crate in your car and one in your home. The home crate
should be close enough to the action that your dog feels included but not
so close that he feels overwhelmed. Before he is housetrained, it's helpful to
furnish a crate for him to sleep in next to your bed so that you can bring him
out whenever he whines to potty during the night. Furnish every crate with soft,
substantial blankets, equally comfortable towels, or crate pads so that your
Poodle remains comfortable and happy inside his den.

   When selecting the
proper crate for your
Poodle, his adult size is
more important than
his puppy size. The
crate should be at least
6 inches (15 cm) longer
than his projected adult
body and 6 inches (15
cm) higher than his adult
shoulder height for
maximum comfort (while
not being big enough for
him to potty on one side

PUPPY POINTER

One Poodle breeder has an excellent way
to prevent her puppies from chewing on
electrical cords: she covers them with PVC
pipe. Just slip the plug end of the cord
through a length of PVC pipe. The pipe will
cover the exposed cord and protect it from
a curious puppy's teeth. You can also apply
a bitter-tasting (but nontoxic) substance to
discourage chewing, but some puppies lick
that off and chew anyway.

and sleep on the other). If you have a puppy, then while he is growing, block off a portion of each crate so that he cannot create a separate potty area inside.

EXERCISE PENS

While crates get a bad rap, exercise pens offer all the safety of a crate with the ability for your dog to move around and play while he's being confined. Get an exercise pen that's tall enough for your Poodle's projected adult size and sturdy enough that he won't be able to knock it down. Ex-pens can be used during the crazy days of puppyhood and the situations later in life where you would like your Poodle to stay put but want him to have some space to move around in.

For puppies, spread plastic or a waterproof mat underneath indoor exercise pens and well beyond their perimeter so that potty accidents don't penetrate your carpet or floor. On top of the plastic, place a comfortable non-skid mat or those heavy-duty interlocking rubberized tiles to provide a secure surface, and one that's easy for you to clean.

Inside the pen, place a blanket, a ball, a squeaky toy, a wobble board, and a water bowl designed to be difficult to tip over. These are all the furnishings your dog needs for a good time while you prepare dinner, do the laundry, or study for a test. When using outdoor exercise pens, supervise your dog the entire time he's outside.

SUPPLIES FOR YOUR POODLE

FOOD AND WATER

Your breeder will recommend a particular brand of food and nutritious puppy treats or biscuits. Stick with the recommended food for the first several weeks your dog is in his new home. (Make sure this food is high quality, of course, and meets his nutritional needs.) Before changing diets, consult your veterinarian. Always keep fresh water available for your Poodle.

GATES

If exercise pens are the extended version of crates, then baby gates turn whole rooms into exercise pens. Whether your Poodle has his sights on your shoes and you want to keep him out of the hallway or you need him to stay in the living room while you bring furniture up the stairs, gates restrict him from certain areas but give him full range of the house otherwise. They can also help you keep your puppy by your side during housetraining, your senior Poodle with arthritis or reduced vision safely away from the stairs, and your dog of any age on the right track during hide-and-seek.

GROOMING SUPPLIES

No matter which variety of Poodle you are sharing your life with, expect to spend quite a bit of time grooming him. See Chapter 5 for a list of grooming supplies to keep available. Grooming extends beyond the coat, of course, to include dental care, nail care, and more, and many of the necessary supplies are dog-specific. With the right grooming stockroom (or closet) assembled, you'll be ready for rewarding hands-on time with your Poodle.

IDENTIFICATION

Give your Poodle an ID tag on his collar with his name, your name, and your telephone number. Make sure to update the collar tag, of course, whenever you change your number. An additional option for identification is the microchip. This is a small chip implanted between your Poodle's shoulder blades that tells animal shelters or

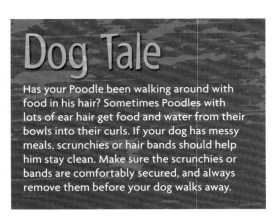

Dog Tale

Has your Poodle been walking around with food in his hair? Sometimes Poodles with lots of ear hair get food and water from their bowls into their curls. If your dog has messy meals, scrunchies or hair bands should help him stay clean. Make sure the scrunchies or bands are comfortably secured, and always remove them before your dog walks away.

veterinarians who scan the chip who you are, where you live, and how to contact you. Updating the microchip is as simple as calling your dog's microchip data registry and changing his information.

LEASHES

You could purchase a 6-foot (2-m) nylon leash (called a "lead" by many trainers) that matches the collar. However, getting a leather leash will give you a durable, long-lasting option that is easier on the hands and won't fray. Hands-free leashes are also useful, whether for jogging or keeping your puppy by your side during housetraining.

Retractable leashes seem useful, but they are not recommended by many trainers. While they allow your Poodle more freedom when they're extended, that extra space makes it more difficult for you to save him if he goes somewhere unsafe or unwanted. Also, when your dog is running to the end of the leash and gathering speed, he could hurt his neck when it stops short, which is less likely with a dog who trots to the end of a 6-foot (2-m) leash. Moreover, the relatively thin cord has also been said to break with enough pressure.

TOYS

Dogs are like kids, and even relatively serene kids, like Poodles, love toys. Toys provide fun times when your dog wants something to do. They also give him something to call his own in a world full of remotes, shoes, and briefcases that he's not supposed to play with. What appeals to your Poodle one day, however, may be ignored the next. Therefore, you should buy your dog various toys, taking some away when he gets bored with them and giving them back in a week or two so that they seem new again.

Beyond giving him different toys, you should provide different kinds, which offer different benefits for both you and your Poodle. Distraction toys, which include chew toys, food toys (which can be stuffed with snacks), squeaky toys, and puzzle toys, give your dog a project and often satisfy his need to chew. Stuffed animals give him someone around the house to cuddle and become friends with when you're gone. Interactive toys facilitate playtime, whether you're tugging rope toys, throwing and catching the flying disc, or just playing fetch with a brand-new tennis ball.

CHAPTER 4

FEEDING YOUR POODLE

Deciding what to serve your Poodle for lunch or dinner seems like a daunting task, but it really isn't. Nationally known dog food companies have been producing premium diets for America's dogs for years. They hire dietitians and veterinarians to design their products, conduct food trials, and monitor the results. The labels on dog food are more explicit than those on baby food.

Good nutrition is the basis of good health. It makes your dog look good and feel good. Good food nourishes his coat, brightens his eyes, sharpens his mind, and puts a spring in his step. Left to his own devices, your Poodle might be rooting in the trash, stealing your Twinkies, or eating squirrels. But you can do better for him than this.

Still, it seems confusing. However, with a little knowledge about the basics of good canine nutrition, you can make an informed choice. You can find a food that fits both your pocketbook and your Poodle's palate.

BASIC NUTRIENTS

The basics of nutrition are simple: protein, fat, carbohydrates, vitamins, and minerals. Along with water, that about covers it. These groupings, of course, contain multitudes, and it helps to learn about each category before buying that next meal.

PROTEINS

Proteins are the workhorses of your dog's diet. They are complex molecules made from various amino acids, 10 of which are called "essential amino acids," because they must be provided in your dog's diet. These are arginine, histidine, isoleucine, leucine, lysine, methionine, phenylalanine, threonine, tryphhtophan, and valine. If even one of them is absent from the diet, important proteins can't be made effectively.

BE AWARE!

Veterinarians often recommend providing more omega-6 fatty acid than omega-3 in your dog's diet. Commonly recommended ratios are 10:1 and 5:1. However, many pet foods are criticized for containing too much omega-6 and not enough omega-3. Consider further research and consult your veterinarian to see what's best for your Poodle.

Proteins are critical for growth, reproduction, and repair. They not only build muscle and aid the immune system but also contribute to the hair and coat. In fact, up to 30 percent of the protein your dog takes in goes into those fabulous Poodle curls. The highest-quality protein comes from meat, eggs, and dairy. High-quality animal protein should be the first ingredient in any commercial dog food. (Raw animal foods, such as raw eggs and fish, should be avoided, but see this chapter's section on raw diets for some perspective.)

FATS

Fats provide energy in a concentrated form with twice the calories of proteins or carbohydrates and supply fatty acids. Just as there are essential amino acids, there are essential fatty acids that your dog needs in his diet. These include linoleic acid and linolenic acid. The former, an omega-6 fatty acid, helps maintain your dog's skin and coat. The latter, an omega-3 fatty acid, helps heal inflammation. Fats also help your dog's body absorb the fat-soluble vitamins A, D, E, and K. Most importantly from your Poodle's point of view, they taste good.

CARBOHYDRATES

Dogs don't need carbohydrates. They can manufacture plenty of energy from fats and proteins alone. However, dogs do have enzymes specifically designed for digesting the carbohydrates starch and sugar, so they can make use of them. Carbohydrates break down easily in their system and can provide quick energy. They comprise between 30 and 70 percent of many commercial dry foods, mostly because they are less expensive energy sources than fats and proteins.

One especially valuable kind of carbohydrate is fiber. Common fibers include cellulose, hemicellulose, pectin, lignin, and gums. While they generally aren't broken down for sustenance in your dog's body, they can help improve digestion and support the proper bacterial mixture in his small intestine.

In cheaper dog foods, carbs are the main source of calories. Better foods have higher amounts of protein and fat. Carbohydrates are found mostly in grains and vegetables, which are not something wild dogs eat much of. Complex carbohydrates like grains must be cooked before a dog can make use of them. (The same is true for us!)

VITAMINS

Vitamins are organic substances that act as catalysts for enzyme reactions. Most vitamins have to be supplied in the diet, as they cannot be synthesized in the body. Unless your veterinarian directs you to, however, it is unnecessary and even dangerous to give your dog vitamin supplements. Vitamins A and D are especially dangerous in large doses. Too much vitamin A can cause bone or joint pain, bone weakness, and even dry skin. Excess vitamin D, on the other hand, can make bones overly dense and may produce soft-tissue and joint calcification.

MINERALS

Minerals are inorganic substances. They are not metabolized, provide no energy, and make up less than 1 percent of your Poodle's body weight. However, they are critical structural components, especially for strong teeth and bones. Macrominerals, which your dog needs in comparatively large amounts, include calcium (Ca), chloride (Cl), magnesium (Mg), phosphorus (P), potassium (K), sodium (Na), and sulfur (S). Trace minerals, which your dog needs less of, include chromium (Cr), copper (Cu), fluorine (F), iodine (I), iron (Fe), manganese (Mn), selenium (Se), and zinc (Zn).

WATER

Most of your Poodle is water, and to keep it that way, your dog needs access to fresh water at all times. It is critical for dozens of physiological functions. Never withhold water in an attempt to make housetraining easier for yourself. Even a 10 percent loss of water can cause serious problems, and a 15 percent loss can kill

Fresh water must always be available to your Poodle.

your dog. Your Poodle does not need to drink Voss. Tap water is fine. Just make sure it is always available.

Water is especially important during strenuous exercise to help prevent dehydration, but in these cases, it should be limited to small amounts given frequently. This will reduce your dog's chances of getting bloat from drinking too much water too quickly.

WHAT TO FEED YOUR POODLE

Unless your vet recommends otherwise, an adult Poodle should be fed twice a day. While dogs seem to prefer home-cooked or canned food (which usually have higher fat content than dry food), a high-quality commercial kibble provides your dog with what he needs. And of course, kibble's economy and convenience have led to its popularity among owners. In any case, measure the food carefully so that you actually know how much you are giving your Poodle. If you have more than one dog, feed them separately. Keep the food bowls clean, and discard uneaten food.

While the occasional appropriate snack will not hurt your Poodle, you should never offer him chocolate, grapes, raisins, alcohol, macadamia nuts, anything containing xylitol, candy, milk, onions, garlic, or avocado leaves, stems, skin, or pits. These are among the human foods that are toxic to dogs. Check online for the safety of other foods that aren't labeled for dogs before sharing them with yours. (Fruit pits and seeds are often toxic too, even when the fruits themselves are okay.) Even foods that aren't specifically poisonous to dogs may have unhealthy levels of fat or other nutrients.

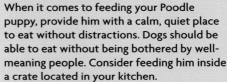

PUPPY POINTER

When it comes to feeding your Poodle puppy, provide him with a calm, quiet place to eat without distractions. Dogs should be able to eat without being bothered by well-meaning people. Consider feeding him inside a crate located in your kitchen.

When he has finished eating, take him out immediately. Don't make a puppy wait. When food reaches your puppy's stomach, his intestines will be stimulated and he will not be able to help himself. Especially in the beginning stages of housetraining, make him successful by anticipating his needs. You'll find that he may play a bit after his after-feeding potty trip, and then he will sleep. After his nap, take your puppy outside again. While waking and immediately after meals are times puppies normally want to relieve themselves.

COMMERCIAL FOODS

Commercial dog foods come in many forms. The most common are dry (kibble), canned, and semi-moist. As mentioned before, dry food is often your best bet for solid, consistent nutrition. It doesn't easily spoil, is formulated to be a complete diet, and makes financial sense—one big bag and you're good to go. Canned food, while often tastier to dogs and more obviously containing meat, goes bad more easily, is more expensive than dry food, and contributes more readily to tooth decay without regular brushing.

Semi-moist food is your Poodle's least healthy option. While it usually lasts longer in the pantry than canned food, it often contains various preservatives, artificial ingredients, and sweeteners, is relatively expensive, and contributes even more readily to tooth decay. Semi-moist food makes for a tasty treat every so often but not for a healthy diet.

While dry diets are often recommended most highly, some dog owners mix canned food into their dog's kibble for a tasty treat every once in a while. No matter what kind seems best, it's up to you to choose a healthy and complete dog food. Good dog food companies (usually the larger national brands) employ animal nutritionists and veterinary scientists to develop their products, conduct regular quality tests and feeding trials, and test raw materials for impurities. While

they may not be privy to the whole process, wise dog owners research brands and check every package for three things when shopping for commercial food: the AAFCO statement, the ingredients, and the guaranteed analysis.

The AAFCO Statement

Choosing a commercial dog food should be done carefully. Once chosen, your Poodle's dog food will probably constitute most of his diet. Luckily, you'll have some help from the Association of American Feed Control Officials (AAFCO) and the National Research Council (NRC) in choosing something that meets basic nutritional standards.

Foods that are nutritionally adequate will have the AAFCO statement on the back of the package. This statement means that the diet follows the requirements set by the NRC for canine nutrition. If no AAFCO designation appears, do not consider this diet for your dog. (Those interested in more detail should search online for AAFCO's nutrient profiles for dog food. Cat owners can also find their nutrient profiles for cat food.)

Of course, the AAFCO statement doesn't mean that a given food is the healthiest possible choice for your dog. There's more research to do. First consider life stage when deciding what constitutes nutritional completeness. Puppies, adults, and senior dogs have different requirements for calories, protein-to-fat ratios, and other nutritional factors. Requirements also vary based on a Poodle's individual needs considering current weight, activity level, and health status. For example, your Poodle puppy needs more protein and fat than he will when he grows into adulthood.

The Ingredients

Dog food manufacturers are required to list all of a product's ingredients in descending order of their precooking weights. When you examine the content label, a high-quality meat protein should be listed at or near the very top. Poor commercial dog foods tend to contain less meat, more meat by-products, and anonymous meat ingredients. You want named proteins, such as chicken, duck, or

Diets with fewer ingredients and no additives generally will be labeled "organic" or "natural," which mean different things.

salmon. Better foods might also contain vegetables and should have a relatively small proportion of grains.

Checking out the ingredients can also help you avoid toxins. The term "toxins" means not only poor-quality or fouled ingredients but also those that create an allergic reaction. In general, the fewer ingredients your dog's diet has, the better. Excess baggage often means additives, which cause problems for many dogs. Additives include artificial coloring (your Poodle doesn't care about color; he cares about smell and, to a lesser extent, taste), artificial flavoring (the flavor should be in the ingredients), artificial preservatives, and chemicals used with efficiency and economy rather than your Poodle's health in mind.

Diets with fewer ingredients and no additives generally will be labeled "organic" or "natural." Organic diets are free of ingredients grown with pesticides, hormones, or agricultural or livestock practices that do not meet strict standards. "Natural," however, is a marketing designation that does not come with standards that must be met. While the ingredients in "natural" foods generally do not meet organic standards, their manufacturers may have formulated these diets with as few additives as possible.

The Guaranteed Analysis

The back of each dog food package has a guaranteed analysis showing what percentage of the food comes from which nutrients. Because this chart includes the moisture content, it's not always easy to estimate how much of each nutrient your Poodle is getting. Water may constitute 70 percent of your canned food. That might make kibble (which is often 6 to 10 percent water) look like it contains more protein, because the canned food's high moisture percentage makes the other percentages appear low. While dogs eating wet food may indeed have to consume more to obtain the same nutrition as a smaller amount of kibble, this difference obscures the comparison between dry and canned foods.

Comparing foods on a dry-matter basis removes water from the equation and tells you what percentage of the actual food in the package is your given nutrient. Just divide the percentage of the nutrient you want to compare (say, protein) by the total percentage of the food's dry matter (which can be found by subtracting the moisture percentage from 100). Multiply the quotient by 100 and you have your percentage. With food that's 75 percent moisture and 14 percent protein, 56 percent of the dry matter is protein. While moisture still plays into what your dog is eating and how nutritious it is, comparing food on a dry-matter basis can give you a better idea of how the different choices relate.

Noncommercial diets have various benefits, but they should be planned with professional guidance.

NONCOMMERCIAL FOODS

In the old days, there was no "dog food." Dogs got human leftovers f they were lucky. Many dogs presumably did quite well on such handouts, as they are scavengers by nature. Even sophisticated Poodles were once scavengers, although it is not polite to remind them of this inconvenient fact.

Home-Cooked Diets

Many dog owners cook meals specifically for their dogs. They are sometimes driven to do this because of their dog's intolerance to something in a commercial diet, but other people might just want to prepare special meals for their Poodle.

Home cooking for your dog can be an excellent practice if you are sure you are providing a nutritionally complete diet. Since dogs have different nutritional needs than we do, this is not the realm for guesswork. People preparing these diets should consult a veterinary nutritionist (or purchase a book written by one) for healthful recipes. Typical ingredients may include lean poultry, ground beef, fish, cooked whole grains, boiled, sauceless pasta, eggs, steamed or raw veggies, cheese, yogurt, peanut butter (without xylitol), and so on. Home chefs must always check their ingredients before serving them, however. Many human foods that seem innocuous and even healthy can be highly toxic to dogs. These include onions, garlic, grapes, raisins, and many others.

Most dogs don't need supplements, which should be given only with specific veterinary guidance.

Raw Diets

The raw diet is a great favorite among some pet owners unconcerned with salmonella. Racing Greyhounds and sled dog have been eating them for generations. Promoters of raw diets say their dogs have shinier coats, cleaner teeth, and more energy. Typical foods include muscle meat (often attached to the bone), ground or whole bones, organ meats, raw eggs, vegetables, and some dairy.

Dogs like raw diets (although taste tests show that some prefer lightly cooked food), but there are downsides. Beyond presenting a higher possibility of food poisoning, raw diets require good planning to make sure they are nutritionally adequate. Feeding a dog only meat, for example, will cause a severe mineral imbalance, so the calcium found in ground bones will be essential. (Never feed your Poodle cooked bones, however, because they can splinter and cause serious internal damage. This can cause injury or death.) Another disadvantage of the raw diet is cost, which can be two or three times that of a super-premium commercial diet. But many dogs do like this diet.

SPECIAL DIETS

Managing your Poodle's diet can help prevent or stabilize many diseases and improve his quality of life. Dogs with serious illnesses may need prescription diets, available from your veterinarian, that support their special needs. These can be costly. However, their benefit is improved health for your pet, and that usually means fewer vet visits. Diet won't necessarily cure chronic kidney disease, but your dog may be kept in better health for longer with prescription diets.

SUPPLEMENTS

Most dogs don't need supplements. A well-balanced diet is supplemented enough, and excess nutrients can actually be harmful, especially to puppies. Unless your veterinarian specifically recommends a specific supplement for a specific reason, avoid them.

TREATS

Dogs like treats. While Poodles will love most treats, they are best served more nutritious options, like slices of carrot or apple (without the seeds, which, like many fruit seeds and pits, are toxic), healthy biscuits, or a bit of peanut butter. With these treats and others, the key word is moderation. Your Poodle must watch his waistline.

Though it's a canine favorite that is considered healthy in moderation, peanut butter is sometimes made with xylitol, a sweetener that is highly toxic to dogs.

Overweight dogs are at increased risk for various conditions. Check your dog to make sure he's at a healthy weight.

Always check the label to make sure that your peanut butter doesn't have this or other harmful ingredients before sharing some with your dog.

BONES AND RAWHIDE

Don't give your Poodle cooked bones. Don't give him rawhide either. Cooked bones can get stuck in your dog's throat or puncture his intestines. Rawhide can cause choking or intestinal blockage, may be contaminated with bacteria like salmonella or *E. coli*, and may cause allergic reactions. Your Poodle does not need to risk his life chewing these hazardous materials. Give him a chew toy instead.

WHEN TO FEED YOUR POODLE

Most dogs do best with twice-a-day feeding, while dogs with certain medical conditions require more frequent meals. Toy breeds should also be fed more frequently each day so that they don't develop hypoglycemia, or low blood sugar. Once-a-day feeding for any dog can cause stress and health problems (larger dogs are susceptible to bloat, for example). However often you feed your dog, try to make it consistent. Dogs like schedules, and knowing when to expect the next meal makes them calmer and less anxious.

So-called free-feeding, or leaving food out all day, is a bad idea, especially if you own more than one dog. You never know if both of them are eating enough. In addition, dogs who eat on a schedule poop on a schedule. If you need another reason, leaving a dish of food around on the floor is a formal invitation to rats and mice. However, you should always keep fresh water available for your Poodle.

OBESITY

Obesity is a major concern for dogs. Even if your dog's weight isn't currently a concern, keep an eye on his body condition. While Poodles are naturally elegant in figure, overfeeding can turn your svelte Poodle into a waddling creature no one would associate with haute couture. This is especially true for older dogs. As they age, they require fewer calories, even though they typically want to eat just as much. Unfortunately, most also exercise less, which compounds the problem.

Overweight dogs have little or no discernible waist and may often pack some fat in the lumbar region above the tail. If you can't readily feel every rib (mild padding is normal), your dog is overweight. Overweight dogs are at increased risk for cancer, diabetes, heart disease, hypertension, arthritis, and bladder stones. Such dogs are often less tolerant to anesthesia. There is just no advantage to it.

Generally your vet will put your dog on a diet rich in protein and fiber but low in fat. She will also suggest gradually increasing his exercise as much as his condition will allow. Bringing in too much exercise too quickly can be stressful and harmful to your dog.

GROOMING
YOUR POODLE

When someone asks, "How much grooming does a Poodle need?" or "How much grooming will I have to do?" the answer is, "It depends." Grooming needs generally depend on your lifestyle and the activities that you and your Poodle enjoy.

Are you showing your Poodle in conformation? You're going to become an expert and spend substantial time grooming him every day to keep his coat in top condition. Do you just want to keep him in a short pet clip? You can brush and comb him when you like and take him to a groomer every four to six weeks.

WHY GROOMING IS IMPORTANT

Grooming is where health care hits home. It comprises some of the most important support you'll provide for your Poodle. Not only is his coat his most distinctive feature, but along with his teeth, skin, ears, eyes, and nails, it is a significant portion of his body that needs to be maintained. Grooming also allows you to check your Poodle for signs of illness and unrest. When done with love, it offers excellent bonding time as well.

Grooming comes in handy for various situations. If you and your Poodle hike and participate in field trials, you'll groom him when he needs the mud and dust of sport removed. Frequent brushing and combing will be necessary to check for ticks and burrs and remove uncomfortable mats. If you're crazy about styling and adore grooming as another mode of artistic expression, you're going to groom your Poodle every day to maintain the illusion that he is really a panda bear.

GROOMING SUPPLIES

Grooming is made easier, even possible, with the right supplies. The following supplies comprise everything you'll need for your dog's grooming routine. Refer back to this list with any questions about what kinds of supplies to use.
- **Bristle brush:** A softer brush that works well where hair is clipped short.
- **Cotton balls:** You'll need cotton balls to protect your Poodle's ears from water, shampoo, and other products during bathing.
- **Dog toothbrush:** Toothbrushes for dogs often have special shapes to more easily traverse your dog's mouth.
- **Dog toothpaste:** Made with great flavors like poultry and seafood, canine-specific toothpaste is safe for dogs. Never use human toothpaste, which can be harmful to your pet.
- **Ear-cleaning-and-drying solution:** Should be mild, alcohol-free, and made for dogs. Harsh cleaners and alcohol can be painful and irritate the tissue, creating more problems.

Groomers are important service providers for Poodle owners.

- **Finger brush or dental wipes:** These toothbrush alternatives may be more acceptable to some dogs.
- **Gauze:** Used for ear and eye cleaning. Do not use cotton swabs for ear cleaning, because they can damage your dog's ears.
- **Greyhound comb:** Combs are used after brushing. The steel Greyhound comb has widely spaced teeth at one end and more closely spaced teeth at the other.
- **Grooming scissors:** Used for trimming excess hair around the eyes.
- **Grooming table:** Helpful for many grooming processes, the grooming table allows you to stand up while giving your Poodle cosmetic attention. Always supervise him while he's on the table so that he doesn't jump or fall off, which could hurt his legs. Some grooming tables have attachments for leashes, but these are hazardous because your dog could be seriously hurt if he jumps from the table while leashed.
- **Guillotine- or scissors-style clipper:** Used to trim the nails. A grinding device is not recommended for your Poodle, because the hair on his feet can become entwined with the spinning mechanism, causing a painful episode.
- **Handheld spray unit:** Allows you to thoroughly wet and rinse your Poodle's coat during baths.
- **Nail file:** Use a coarse- with smooth-sided nail file to smooth any roughness created by trimming the nails.

GROOMING YOUR POODLE

- **Premoistened eye wipes:** Used to remove tearstains. Alternatively, you could use a dilute solution of hydrogen peroxide and water (1:10).
- **Shampoo and conditioner:** Shampoo and conditioner are used during baths. Use conditioner if your Poodle has dry skin or hair (get oil-based conditioner or keep coat oil on hand to mix in). Always use products made for dogs.
- **Slicker brush:** Used for getting through thick coats. Should have short wire tines.
- **Stand dryer:** Leaves both hands free to brush and comb your Poodle while you dry him. If you're going to bathe and groom your dog yourself, spend the money for this appliance. Never leave your Poodle unattended or confined while being dried. Stop drying him if he shows discomfort.
- **Sterile veterinary eyewash:** Used for eye cleaning.
- **Styptic pencil or powder:** Used to stop the bleeding if you nip the quick during nail trimming.
- **Towels:** Used for drying off your dog before you leave the tub.
- **Treats:** These help your dog stay enthusiastic about various grooming processes. Choose healthy treats!
- **Waterproof apron:** You may wish to wear this to keep your clothes dry while bathing your Poodle.

TO GROOM OR TO GROOMER? THAT IS THE QUESTION

Poodle owners can choose to do all the grooming themselves, some of the grooming, or practically no grooming. If you have your Poodle in a show coat, you will need to brush and comb him every day. But for pet clips (those not meant for exhibition), longtime Poodle people say the perceived need for daily grooming is overblown (pun intended).

Experts with 40 years' experience say that with the breed in a pet clip, sensible people don't groom much between visits to the Poodle parlor for a bath, clip, and groom. Other experts suggest you brush your Poodle several times each week and remove tangles. Everyone does agree on this much: the shorter the coat, the less grooming is required.

For some people, any grooming is too much—either the time required is too much or the task isn't something they want to do. For many people willing to brush and comb, the bath and clip are too much. Apartment dwellers don't have the room for a grooming table or the accoutrements for the full treatment. That's why groomers today are, as they were in the past, important service providers for Poodle owners.

FINDING AN EXPERIENCED GROOMER

A good groomer is worth her weight in gold. She not only knows what your dog's finished coat should look like and can do the job efficiently, but she also loves dogs and knows how to keep your Poodle comfortable and calm. Once a dog has a difficult or unpleasant grooming experience, future groomers will have quite a job helping him put that experience behind him.

PUPPY POINTER

Since grooming is a significant part of your Poodle's life, beginning early is important. Ask your breeder about your puppy's grooming experience. A good breeder will have handled your puppy daily since birth. She will likely have clipped his face at least twice and other sections of his coat at least once, rewarding his compliance with a meaty treat. In other words, your puppy may have come to you with weeks of grooming experience, the brushes, combs, and clippers already familiar to him. With this experience already in place, you need only reinforce good grooming behavior with treats.

Many people call themselves professional groomers. Selecting from the approximately 85,000 grooming businesses in the United States (with another 8,000 in Canada) begins with location. Within a reasonable distance of your home, how do you separate the good groomers from the not-so-good in a profession that has few guidelines? You can do the research and perhaps avoid a difficult experience if you know what questions to ask.

Your breeder, members of your nearest Poodle club, and your veterinarian should have the knowledge to point you in the right direction. Start with their recommendations, visiting each candidate groomer's shop. Notice in particular how clean the grooming facility is and how comfortable the pets seem. Ascertain which bathing and finishing products each groomer uses and why she chose those brands. Also ask about where the staff were trained and how much grooming experience they have.

When you talk with prospective groomers, show them a photograph of a Poodle in your desired trim. Ask about the cost. Also discuss the procedure each groomer follows, which tools she uses, and the extent of her grooming (for example, the length of the clip on the body versus the feet and face). When you have visited several of the recommended groomers, you will have an opinion about which will work best for your Poodle.

THE GROOMING APPOINTMENT

When you bring your Poodle in for his appointment, again discuss the procedure your groomer will follow and the extent of her grooming plans, along with any particulars that are important to you. Leave the picture (or a copy of the picture) of the finish that you want. That way, your expectations are clear.

Good grooming should be a companionable collaboration between your groomer, your dog, and yourself. Does your Poodle resist certain grooming routines? Inform your groomer in advance. After the grooming is done, question her about how your Poodle handed the different parts of the process. Does your Poodle not gel with your groomer? Keep looking. The most important things are planning your grooming goals and working with groomers until you and your Poodle are happy with the outcome.

SELECTING THE RIGHT CLIP

The clip that works best for your Poodle depends on his activities, habits, body type, age, and physical condition. If you do not plan to show your dog in conformation events, you will have more varieties to choose from.

CASUAL CLIPS

Casual Poodle clips can be whatever you want, which often means easier maintenance. Most owners prefer the lamb trim, sometimes called the curly clip. It's close on the body and a bit longer on the legs, leaving a moderate topknot, tail pompon, and ear fringe. Standard Poodle–breeder Eileen Geeson suggests the sporting (or "utility") trim, which is similar to the lamb but closer on the legs, leaving the bracelets slightly longer. If you are a fan of the grooming shows on television and want to experiment with color and clips, learn some basic clips first and then move on to the more complicated Poodle hairdos.

SHOW-RING CLIPS

The following styles are accepted at dog show events. If you have plans to exhibit your dog but don't have great grooming skills, find a groomer experienced in preparing Poodle coats for the show ring. A poor grooming job can create long-lasting havoc for your Poodle's campaign.

The American Kennel Club (AKC) breed standard is very specific about the clip styles required for competition. Poodles over one year old must have the English Saddle or the Continental clip. (Corded coats are also acceptable.) Younger Poodles may be exhibited in the Puppy clip. The Stud Dog and Brood Bitch classes and noncompetitive Parade of Champions events allow Poodles to wear the Sporting clip.

The following summaries have been adapted from the AKC breed standard, which describes these clips (along with coat quality) slightly more precisely. Of course, pet owners need not adhere to any of the official guidelines that follow.

Continental Clip
The face, throat, feet, legs, hindquarters, and base of the tail should be shaved. Pompons may be left on the hips. Bracelets on the hind legs and puffs on the forelegs remain, along with a pompon at the end of the tail. Otherwise, the coat remains full.

English Saddle Clip
The face, throat, feet, forelegs, and base of the tail should be shaved. The hindquarters should be shaved down to a short covering of hair; a curved area from each flank and two bands from each hind leg should be shaved. Puffs should remain on the forelegs, a pompon at the end of the tail. Otherwise, the coat remains full.

Puppy Clip
The face, throat, feet, and base of the tail should be shaved. A pompon is left at the end of the tail. Groomers may shape the coat for greater neatness and a smooth, unbroken line.

Sporting Clip
The face, feet, throat, and base of the tail are shaved. A scissored cap remains on the top of the head, a pompon at the end of the tail. The rest of the coat should be clipped to 1 inch (2.5 cm) or less in length. Slightly longer hair on the legs is acceptable.

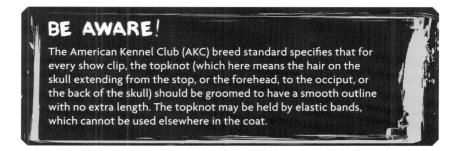

BE AWARE!

The American Kennel Club (AKC) breed standard specifies that for every show clip, the topknot (which here means the hair on the skull extending from the stop, or the forehead, to the occiput, or the back of the skull) should be groomed to have a smooth outline with no extra length. The topknot may be held by elastic bands, which cannot be used elsewhere in the coat.

CORDED COATS

Poodles are not always combed and clipped. Sometimes their coats are allowed to grow long. With proper care, as Poodle hair grows, it twists on itself, producing pencil-width coils called cords. Corded coats came into vogue during the 1890s but fell out of favor because the cords were hard to maintain. You will sometimes see Poodles exhibited in corded coats, creating interest and excitement because of their rarity. According to the AKC

The clip that works best for your Poodle depends on his activities, habits, body type, age, and physical condition.

breed standard, the cords should be tight and even but their length should differ across the body.

A CONVENIENT GROOMING AREA

Throughout his lifetime, your Poodle will need what many Poodle people call a "fluff and puff" (a bath, dry, comb-out, clip, and shape) every four to six weeks at least. For people with a bit of patience who have room for the right equipment, learning to groom your own Poodle can be enjoyable and is more economical than buying the grooming service. You invest in the tools and set aside the time and grooming becomes part of your ritual.

If you do decide to take care of your Poodle's grooming yourself, consider creating an area in your home dedicated to the task. Make it convenient, pleasant, and attractive for you and your dog. Keep your tools stored at hand so that your task goes more quickly. Keep a supply of favored treats nearby so you can reward your Poodle for getting up and staying on the grooming table. And your back will thank you for installing a table at the proper height.

BRUSHING

For Poodles in full coats brushing and combing are an absolute necessity—if not each day, then certainly every other day. Poodles' beautiful long coats become increasingly matted and soiled if they are not cared for on a regular basis. Poodles with pet clips also benefit from regular brushing and combing.

HOW TO BRUSH YOUR POODLE

There are many right ways to groom a Poodle. However, you and your dog will work most efficiently if you stick to a system. If you're a beginner, start with the system described below, suggested by Standard Poodle–breeder Eileen Geeson. As you develop experience, spend time with other Poodle people, and perhaps attend a seminar or two, you'll develop your own system.

While your Poodle is standing on the grooming table, follow these steps:

1. Start with the head. Brush away from the eyes and down the ears. Brush the hair behind the ears where tangling is easy.
2. Brush down the neck and along the body toward the tail.
3. Brush the tail.
4. Now groom the right foreleg. From the toes, brush upward toward the ribs. Then, starting from the bottom, section the hair and comb through each layer to the skin. Do the right hind leg following the same pattern. Be sure to brush thoroughly under the foreleg (in the armpits) and inside the legs.
5. Turn your dog. Give your command, *turn*, each time he turns so that he learns what's expected and to turn on command. Treat after you give the command. (See Chapter 7 for more information on command training.)
6. Repeat step four with the other front and hind leg. As you did before, part each section of long hair and comb to the skin.

BATHING

Your Poodle needs baths just like you do. Bathing washes away weeks of accumulated grime, rejuvenating your dog's skin and coat. It's also necessary for getting good results when your dog is clipped. If you have an area with a

BE AWARE!

Brushing not only helps keep your dog looking good but is essential to the health of his skin and coat. Especially in those places where your Poodle's skin folds, such as under the legs and behind the ears, everyday rubbing causes tangling and matting of the hair. When the hair mats, the amount of rubbing increases, causing tenderness in the skin.

grooming table and tub, that's ideal. You could also visit a grooming parlor that provides dog washing and grooming facilities that customers can use for a fee. Bathe your Poodle every six to eight weeks, more often if he gets dirty and needs another bath in between.

Always bathe your Poodle in a warm environment. Being bathed outside, for example, could be uncomfortable and unhealthy for your damp, stationary dog. This is especially true for very young or old pets, who are more likely to be adversely affected by the cold. When bathing your dog, use slightly warm water. No matter what tub you use, place a skidproof mat on the bottom.

HOW TO BATHE YOUR POODLE

Experience will advise whether your Poodle needs you to groom out his mats and tangles before bath time (antitangle spray can be helpful) or if you're better off detangling his coat by hand while bathing him. Ask your breeder when she thinks addressing tangles and mats would be most comfortable and efficient.

Depending on your Poodle's size, the height of your tub, and your abilities, you can either use a ramp to get him into the bathtub or lift him over the side. If you're lifting him, hold him around the chest and back legs and lower him in. Regardless of location or mode of tub entry, make sure he stands still during the bath. Bathing should be enjoyable for your dog and makes for great bonding time, but it requires cooperation.

Note: Remember to use canine-specific shampoo and conditioner. Dog skin and hair are different from ours, and you will want products that cater to those differences. Human hair products can be harmful to dogs.

1. Wet your Poodle's coat thoroughly with warm water. Using your handheld spray unit, start with the base of the body and work upward so that the water penetrates rather than runs off the coat. Place cotton balls just inside both ears to help prevent water and shampoo from entering the ear canals.

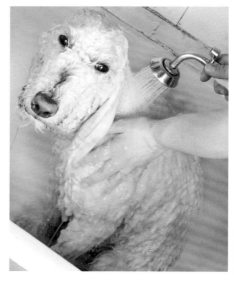

Bathing is necessary for getting good results from clipping and trimming.

2. Distribute the shampoo over the head and body, down the legs, and down the tail. Then lather. Work the shampoo through the coat until you reach the skin. Be sure to bathe your Poodle's underside (including his genitals and under his tail) and inside his ear flaps. Avoid getting shampoo in his eyes.
3. Once your Poodle's coat feels clean, rinse with warm water, starting from his head. Use your hands to direct water and shampoo away from his eyes. Rinse his ear flaps, neck, body, legs, and tail. Rinse underneath, ensuring that each layer of his coat is clean.
4. Rinsing takes time. The saying is, "When you think you've rinsed enough, rinse five minutes more." Double-check to ensure your Poodle's coat is squeaky clean before you begin drying. Some coats require conditioner. If your dog has dry hair or skin, use an oil-based conditioner or add a teaspoon (5 mL) of coat oil to another canine conditioner. Massage the product in and then rinse again.
5. Drying begins inside the tub with towels. Towel your dog dry as well you can. Then move your dog to the grooming table.
6. Turn on the stand dryer. When using the stand dryer, watch your Poodle for discomfort and make sure he doesn't overheat. Never confine him under the heat, and turn the dryer off if he shows signs of distress. Never leave the room while the dryer is running.
7. Begin with the feet and move upward. Brush continuously until each section is dry before going on to the next. Using the system you've established for regular grooming (see "How to Brush Your Poodle"), proceed until the hair is fluffy.
8. When finishing, comb your Poodle's hair using the widely spaced section of the comb to ensure that any tangles are removed. If you fail to brush and comb thoroughly when drying, your Poodle's coat will mat.

EAR CARE

Some Poodles experience hygiene issues arising from a damp atmosphere within the hair growing inside their ears. This may make plucking your dog's ear hair appropriate, but if he doesn't have these issues, plucking may be ill-advised. Many longtime Poodle people believe that you should not mess around with your dog's ears more than you have to.

Many veterinarians say that routine ear cleaning is usually unnecessary. (Of course, some dogs have more ear trouble than others.) Light-brown wax is normal in small amounts. However, if you detect an odor or see any mites, contact your veterinarian. Ear trouble should be addressed immediately to help prevent complications. With good care, it can often be cleared up within the week.

HOW TO GROOM YOUR POODLE'S EARS

Ear cleaning is simple enough, but watch your breeder, veterinarian, or groomer perform the routine safely before trying it at home. If you employ a groomer, she will include ear cleaning as part of the service.

Dog Tale

Dogs with oiled coats collect more dirt and can create havoc with your furniture. Imagine your wandering Poodle leaving a trail wherever he goes! Standard Poodle–breeder Eileen Geeson suggests that you forgo oiling your dog's coat. However, there are many opinions on this topic. Your breeder will know what works well with her breeding line's coats.

1. Clean the inside of the ear flap gently with a cloth or gauze.
2. After being shown how by a qualified professional, clean the ear canal by applying a few drops of a mild, alcohol-free ear-cleaning-and-drying solution, massaging the base of the ear to loosen secretions. Then wipe the ear canal with gauze or cotton balls. Do not use cotton swabs, as these can hurt your dog's ears, push debris further inside the ear canals, and cause ear infections.
3. Give your Poodle a treat to keep him positive about ear cleaning.

EYE CARE

Dogs with long hair around their eyes often experience related irritation. Unfortunately, the tears produced to lubricate their eyes and reduce the irritation cause reddish-brown stains. These are known as tearstains. Tearstaining may occur without apparent irritation; there may simply be an overflow of tears. Given that tearstaining is sometimes called "Poodle eye," you can gather that Poodles are an affected breed.

By carefully clipping the irritating hair—perhaps much more often than you clip the rest of the body—the irritation may be reduced. When the cause is unclear, tearstaining can be reduced through daily cleaning. Never use bleach to remove the stains. Bleach fumes are harmful and the probability of accidental damage to the eyes is a risk foolish to take.

Should your Poodle's eyes appear red or have a wet discharge instead of tears, bring him to the veterinarian. Also bring him in for excessive wetness or tearstaining, which can signal health problems like food allergies, yeast infections, and bacterial infections.

HOW TO GROOM YOUR POODLE'S EYES

1. Wash your hands. If you use a grooming table, place your Poodle onto it.
2. Carefully trim excess hair away from your dog's eyes.
3. Now clean the eyes with sterile veterinary eyewash. First put your dog down on the grooming table and tilt his muzzle up. Then steady the dropper bottle against his head, squeeze the recommended number of drops into each eye, and gently work the eyewash in by moving the skin around the eye.
4. Using a moistened gauze pad, wipe underneath each eye from the inner corner to the outer corner, gently blotting excess eyewash and removing dried mucus.
5. Remove tearstains with either a dilute solution of hydrogen peroxide and water (1:10) or a premoistened eye cleaning towelette.
6. Treat your Poodle to preserve good associations about eye care.

NAIL TRIMMING

Regular nail trimming is important for keeping your Poodle's toes in the proper position and preventing him from catching and tearing a nail. Additionally, without regular trimming, dewclaws that have not been removed can become ingrown, which is painful.

Carefully trim excess hair away from your Poodle's eyes to help prevent irritation.

Dogs who regularly walk, run, and play on rough surfaces need their nails trimmed less often than other dogs do. Generally speaking, if your dog's nails clatter while he walks, it's time for a trim. Keep in mind that if you frequently pick up your dog, he may need a trim halfway between your regular grooming appointments. Otherwise, his nails may become long or rough and unintentionally cause deep scratches in your arms.

HOW TO TRIM YOUR POODLE'S NAILS

Be sure to watch your Poodle's groomer before trimming the nails yourself. It's helpful to be guided once or twice by someone who knows the process well. Once you begin a session, keep a steady pace. You may want to have a friend hold your Poodle steady and hand you things during the early stages of your career as your Poodle's manicurist.

Have a styptic pencil or styptic powder next to the table in case you cut into the quick, a sensitive area inside the nail, and cause bleeding. Trim only the end of the nail to avoid this area. Give your Poodle manicures in a well-lit area so that you can better see the quick in light-colored nails. With darker ones, you may not be able to see it and must be more careful. Consider using a flashlight underneath darker nails during grooming, which may help you ascertain where to stop.

1. Put your Poodle on the grooming table.
2. Hold one of his paws and move any hair away from the nail. Place your finger under the toe.
3. With the clippers, trim the nail parallel to the toe pad.
4. When you're done clipping your dog's nails, file each to eliminate any roughness.
5. Give your dog a treat.

DENTAL CARE

Teeth are an essential part of the digestive system. Since the digestive system processes the nutrients that build your beautiful Poodle and maintain his energy, healthy teeth and gums help keep him feeling good. And just like with humans, regular dental care is necessary to keep those teeth and gums healthy.

Dogs have the same dental hygiene issues that humans have. Without regular brushing, plaque begins to accumulate on their teeth and gumline. When not removed promptly enough, plaque becomes tartar, which can be removed only by your veterinarian.

Plaque and tartar buildup can cause various problems, including gum inflammation, gum recession, bone loss, tooth loss, and even heart disease.

With regular dental care, you can help maintain your Poodle's strong, shiny teeth throughout his life.

However, with regular dental care, you can help prevent these problems and maintain your Poodle's strong, shiny teeth throughout his life.

HOW TO BRUSH YOUR POODLE'S TEETH

Brushing may seem threatening to your Poodle at first. The key to success is to be patient and gradual in your approach. Get your dog used to the process by massaging his teeth with your finger before introducing the toothbrush:

1. Wash your hands. If you use a grooming table, place your Poodle onto it. Otherwise, use a well-lit utility area. Have your Poodle sit. (See Chapter 7 for training instructions.)
2. Rub his teeth and gums gently with your finger in a circular motion. The most important locations are where the teeth meet the gumline.
3. Keep sessions short and positive. Thirty to sixty seconds is enough. Then reward.

When your Poodle becomes comfortable with practice sessions, introduce the toothbrush. He may be wary of this unfamiliar object, so introduce it gradually. Use a finger brush or dental wipes if he has trouble with the standard brush. When your dog accepts brushing, you should brush his teeth once every day.

1. Gather your materials. Have your Poodle sit in his regular practice area.
2. Brush with a soft toothbrush at a 45-degree angle. Always use canine-specific toothpaste, which comes in flavors that dogs love. Human toothpastes contain ingredients that can be harmful when swallowed or inhaled.
3. There's no need to rush. Go at your Poodle's pace and praise him for cooperation.

GROOMING YOUR POODLE

HEALTH OF
YOUR POODLE

Veterinarians are your key partners in caring for your dog.

Everything your Poodle does affects his health. When he scampers and plays, he's getting exercise. When he snoozes on the couch, he's getting rest. When he eats dinner, he's getting nutrition. Everything you've read (and will read) in this book comes together under the headline "Poodle Health." However, keeping your Poodle's health in mind also means knowing which vaccinations he needs, staying well versed on the common inherited diseases that Poodles experience, brushing up on parasite prevention, being ready to provide first aid, and more. These are the subjects you should have covered so that you can get back to everything else.

FINDING A VET

The key player in your Poodle's health care, after you, is your veterinarian. She is your partner in caring for your Poodle. If your breeder has not recommended a veterinarian, check with local Poodle club members. Breed clubs usually keep a list of veterinarians with extensive experience with their breed. In addition, club members will know the various practice personalities. Two other sources of information are the American Veterinary Medical Association (AVMA) (avma.org) and the American Animal Hospital Association (AAHA) (aaha.org).

ANNUAL WELLNESS EXAM

Your dog should have a veterinary wellness exam at least once every year—twice a year when he's a senior. During the exam, your veterinarian will evaluate your dog's physical well-being: how he stands and moves, his weight, his physical condition and temperature, and his eyes and ears, skin tone, heart, lungs, mouth, teeth, genitals, nose, and coat. She may also take a blood sample to check for heartworms and document the results for future comparison. Further tests may be necessary.

Your job is to help by mentioning any problems you may have noticed. Be sure to bring along your dog's vet records if you are switching from another practice and an insurance card if you have pet insurance. You may also be instructed to bring a stool sample, which your vet can check for parasites. Not least, bring any questions that you have for the vet. Discuss any unusual patterns of eating, drinking, eliminating, or behavior you might have noticed. Your Poodle is depending on you to speak for him.

VACCINATIONS

When effective vaccines for distemper and parvovirus were developed, they saved vast numbers of dogs who in previous years would have died from these infections. Additionally, laws requiring rabies vaccinations have almost eliminated canine rabies in the United States.

The American Animal Hospital (AAHA) has developed a list of core (or essential) vaccinations and noncore (or nonessential) vaccinations. These classifications help dog owners stay current on necessary immunizations while knowing which vaccines might not be worth their potential risks. The core vaccines include those for rabies, distemper, adenovirus, and parvovirus. Some noncore vaccines include those for Lyme disease, leptospirosis, and bordetella (commonly known as "kennel cough").

Noncore vaccines can be helpful for certain lifestyles. If your Poodle goes to daycare, a kennel cough vaccine is a must. If your dog works as a retriever, your vet may recommend a Lyme disease vaccine. Because veterinary science advances rapidly, new vaccines frequently become available, but not all of them are necessary, and their risks sometimes outweigh their benefits. Your veterinarian can explain the various vaccine combinations she recommends, and together you can choose what's best for your dog.

ADENOVIRUS

Canine adenovirus comes in two types. While canine adenovirus type 2 (CAV-2) infections generally cause milder respiratory symptoms, canine adenovirus type 1 (CAV-1) infections cause infectious canine hepatitis (ICH), which affects the tonsils, lymph nodes, and then other internal organs, primarily the liver. Milder ICH symptoms include vomiting, diarrhea, and abdominal swelling. Dogs more seriously affected may experience symptoms like high fever, swollen lymph nodes, jaundice, paleness inside the mouth and of the nose, and seizures. Death is uncommon but can occur; otherwise, veterinary care will support affected pets until they recover. "Blue eye," a bluish hazing or clouding of the eyes, occurs in some dogs, most often puppies less than six months old. It generally subsides after recovery, but it can lead to glaucoma or uveitis. The CAV-2 vaccine protects against both canine adenovirus types.

BORDETELLA (KENNEL COUGH)

The contagious lung disease bordetella (one of the conditions known as "kennel cough") is caused by the bacterium *Bordetella bronchiseptica*. Bordetella moves easily through boarding kennels, dog parks, grooming salons, and other canine haunts. Infected dogs make a hacking cough. The disease is usually mild, but puppies and Toy Poodles may require veterinary care to support their breathing and prevent pneumonia. If your Poodle will participate in dog daycare, frequent the dog park,

Your puppy should have his vaccinations completed before going out in public with other dogs.

or be professionally groomed, your veterinarian may recommend a twice-yearly intranasal vaccine or an intramuscular injection of bordetella vaccine.

CORONAVIRUS

Spread through saliva or feces, coronavirus causes symptoms including depression, loss of appetite, vomiting, and yellow-to-orange diarrhea. Because the illness can be treated effectively, vets recommend against vaccination. Coronavirus can be severe in young puppies.

DISTEMPER

Canine distemper is a viral disease that has no known cure. Disseminated through the air and by contact with infected bedding or bowls, it is highly contagious. After residing in the tonsils and lymph nodes for about a week, distemper goes after the respiratory, urogenital, gastrointestinal, and nervous systems. Signs include high fever, lethargy, lack of appetite, dry coughing, vomiting, diarrhea, and seizures.

Distemper is a leading killer of dogs worldwide. Since there is no treatment, vets must rely on supportive therapy, including intravenous fluids and antibiotics to prevent secondary infections. The death rate is very high, and many dogs who recover suffer permanent neurological symptoms. The disease is easily prevented through a series of vaccinations beginning when puppies are six to eight weeks old.

LEPTOSPIROSIS

The term "leptospirosis" refers to the illness commonly transmitted to dogs by one of four bacterial strains from the genus *Leptospira*. Leptospirosis also affects people, pigs, cattle, rats, skunks, opossums, and other animals. Generally, *Leptospira* bacteria are spread through urine, and they can remain in ground water or soil for up to six months. As animals like skunks and opossums appear more and more commonly in the suburbs, the prevalence of leptospirosis seems to be increasing. It is especially common in dogs who spend a lot of time around water or are allowed to drink from standing water or puddles.

Leptospirosis mainly affects the liver and kidneys. Mild cases may produce no symptoms, but serious cases can cause rapid dehydration and require hospitalization. This disease can be fatal. There is a vaccine that protects against the four forms of the disease that commonly affect dogs. Toy Poodles are at some risk for an allergic reaction to the vaccine, and unless your Poodle has an increased risk of exposure, your vet may recommend against vaccination.

LYME DISEASE

Lyme disease is the most common infectious tick-borne illness in the United States. Treatable with antibiotics, it usually begins with sudden lameness, swollen joints, and pain. Kidney and cardiac symptoms are rare but fatal. Tick collars and some flea control products that also kill ticks help reduce the occurrence. Vaccinate only those dogs living in high-risk areas.

PARVOVIRUS

Parvovirus is an extremely contagious viral disease most severely affecting the intestinal tract and white blood cells, especially in puppies 6 to 20 weeks old. In young puppies, the disease may also produce lifelong cardiac problems. Signs include lethargy, foul-smelling stools, and severe vomiting. There is no cure for the disease, and it must be treated with supportive care, including intravenous fluids.

   Parvovirus is easily transmitted by any item that has come into contact with an infected dog's feces, and it can live in the environment for months. (Any areas where an infected dog has lived should be cleaned with a 10 percent bleach solution.) Immunization through a series of vaccinations beginning when puppies are six to eight weeks o d is recommended.

Some vaccinations are necessary for all dogs, but others may not be worth the risk.

RABIES

Rabies is a severe viral infection that affects all mammals. It spreads from the saliva or blood of an infected animal into the bloodstream of the victim through an open wound, usually from a bite from the carrier. It is almost 100 percent fatal. When the virus enters the body, it replicates in muscle cells and then spreads to the nerve fibers, traveling from there to the central nervous system. This can take several weeks, but once the symptoms show, it's already too late. In the first stage, the paralytic rabid stage, the animal may just seem lethargic. As the disease progresses to "furious rabies," however, we see the characteristic foaming of the mouth and aggression.

Human beings can catch rabies from dogs (and vice versa, although that doesn't happen much). That should be enough to convince you to get your dog vaccinated with the highly effective, inexpensive rabies vaccine. In fact, it's against the law in every US state not to. Always bring proof of rabies vaccination (and of other vaccinations) when traveling with your pet.

PARASITES

Although parasites benefit from your Poodle, your Poodle does not benefit from them. In fact, some parasites can endanger your dog's life. These small organisms spread from one animal to another when animals lick or sniff each other or make contact with brush, grass, or feces in which the parasites were deposited.

EXTERNAL PARASITES

External parasites feed on other organisms but live outside their host's body. Beyond causing stress and inconvenience for your dog, they can also cause skin problems and spread disease. Fortunately, most external parasites can be prevented or treated.

Fleas

Fleas proliferate in the warm weather, preferably when it's humid. However, they can remain present as autumn sets in, and your dog can catch them in the backyard or elsewhere, particularly where other animals have been. Once on your dog, adult female fleas begin laying up to 50 eggs each day, which can drop off inside your house. Before long, tiny larvae hatch from the eggs and burrow into carpets, furniture, and soil, where they can be inactive for weeks before emerging as adults looking for a host. The flea life cycle can be as short as 12 days or as long as six months, depending on temperature and humidity.

The most common indication of flea infestation is your dog scratching more than usual. Animals with fleas often also have reddened skin (which sometimes evolves into sores called "hot spots") and telltale reddish-black droppings in their fur called "flea dirt," which is the partially digested blood of your Poodle. Some dogs are so sensitive to flea bites that even one flea may set them scratching and you will see no other signs. In addition to driving your dog crazy, fleas can also carry tapeworm, something else to worry about.

If you have an infestation, treat your dog and your house with vet-recommended flea products. Prevention is easier than treatment, so protect your Poodle by applying a topical flea preventive during flea season, which in many places is all year round. (With modern heating, fleas have found a comfy spot to spend the winter—under your cushions.)

Prevention is easier than treatment for flea infestations.

Mites

Three main types of mites cause dogs pain and suffering: ear mites, sarcoptic mange mites, and demodectic mange mites. Dogs commonly pick up the first kind through close contact with infested pets or bedding. Ear mites cause intense irritation signaled by head shaking and ear scratching, which can cause bleeding sores. Ear-mite infections often cause brown or black discharge; examined under a microscope, this substance can confirm the presence of the parasites. An ear-mite medication combined with ear cleaning can eliminate the issue.

Sarcoptic mange mites cause sarcoptic mange (or "canine scabies"). Highly contagious, sarcoptic mange can affect your Poodle any time of year. Passed by close contact with infected animals, bedding, or grooming tools, these mites burrow through your Poodle's skin, causing intense itching, hair loss, skin irritation, and scabs. Medication can eliminate sarcoptic mange mites, and properly cleaning your Poodle's environment helps prevent reinfection.

Demodectic mange mites are microscopic parasites generally passed from the mother. Since healthy dogs often have them without showing signs of a problem, symptoms often signal further health problems. More common in young dogs, demodectic mange causes lesions around the face, legs, or trunk. The more severe form, generalized demodectic mange, affects the whole body. Medical intervention generally helps, but the generalized form requires more intensive treatment.

Ringworm

When is a worm not a worm? When it's ringworm. Ringworm is a fungal infection found primarily in puppies or younger dogs. This infection creates patches of bald, irritated skin. Transmitted through direct contact, it is highly infectious to people, especially children. Ringworm can be treated with an antifungal medication.

Ticks

Any animal that walks in wooded areas and brush may become a tick's host. Most often found on your dog's neck or ears, in the folds between his legs and body, or between his toes, ticks attach to their host's body and feed for several days. Their bites can cause skin irritation and spread diseases, such as Lyme disease and Rocky Mountain spotted fever. Heavy-enough infestations can cause anemia. However, not all ticks carry disease, and removing them promptly can otherwise prevent infection, which sometimes occurs only after they have been feeding for one to two days.

After camping, sporting, or hiking trips, examine your Poodle. If you find a tick, carefully use tweezers to grip it as close to its head as possible. (Do not grasp the body, which may cause the tick to regurgitate into your Poodle.) Now, gently and steadily, pull the tick free. Drop it into a container of rubbing alcohol and wash your hands. Treat at-risk pets with an appropriate tick preventive. If your backyard breeds ticks, trim bushes and remove brush to reduce your risk of infestation.

BE AWARE!

Internal and external parasites can cause serious problems for you and your dog. Consult your veterinarian if your Poodle shows any symptoms that suggest infestation. Prompt treatment of parasites lessens your dog's discomfort, decreases the chances of disease transmission, and helps rid your home of pests.

Adult dogs generally get hookworms from ingesting contaminated soil, water, or animal tissue.

INTERNAL PARASITES

Internal parasites usually live in your dog's digestive system. Of course, one common exception is the heartworm. Treatment of internal parasites generally requires the destruction of their eggs and larvae as well as the adult worms.

Heartworm

Heartworms live and breed in the heart, where they can become 12 inches (30.5 cm) long as adults. When heartworm infestations become severe enough, they can cause heart, liver, or kidney failure or other fatal complications. However, they may not produce symptoms until the condition worsens. Early symptoms include coughing and fatigue, which can become more pronounced over time.

Heartworm is generally treated with two or three injections of an arsenic-based medication called Immiticide (melarsomine dihydrochloride). Immiticide kills the worms, which then break up into pieces. These pieces can block up the pulmonary vessels and actually kill the dog. The only way to help prevent this catastrophe is to keep the dog confined and quiet during the course of the treatment, which may take several weeks or months.

Heartworm is transmitted by infected mosquitoes and has been documented in every US state. Obviously it is better to make sure your dog is on year-round heartworm prevention for his entire life. It takes only one infected mosquito to kill your dog. Many heartworm medications now protect against other worms, fleas, and ticks as well. Your dog will thank you.

Hookworm

Hookworms are small, thin worms that attach themselves to the inside of the small intestine. Puppies acquire hookworms through their mother's milk. Adult dogs commonly become infected by direct contact with larvae or ingesting them from soil, water, or animal tissue. Hookworm infections may produce no symptoms, but bloody diarrhea, weight loss, and progressive weakness can occur. Diagnosis is through eggs in the feces. When dogs recover, they still carry larvae in their tissues, which can be released during stress or illness.

Hookworms are treated with a dewormer, but they require multiple doses for effective treatment. (Most dewormers only kill the adult worms; they don't hurt the larvae.) A follow-up fecal exam by your vet will determine if all the worms have been destroyed. Most heartworm medications help prevent hookworms.

Roundworm

Roundworms live in the stomach or intestines and can grow as long as 7 inches (18 cm). Females can lay up to 200,000 eggs each day, each protected by a hard shell that allows it to live for months in the soil. Similarly to hookworms, roundworms are contracted by puppies from their mother's milk (or even before birth) and by adult dogs through ingesting contaminated soil or animal tissue. Roundworms can also be transmitted to children, especially those permitted to play in sandboxes, where cats or dogs may have defecated. Children should be encouraged to wash their hands after petting cats or dogs to keep infection rates low.

Signs of roundworm include potbelly, recurrent diarrhea, general weakness, vomiting, dull coat, and weight loss. You may also see the worms in your dog's feces or vomit. Roundworms will also retard your puppy's development. Forms of the parasite occur in the circulatory system, stomach, and intestines. Most worm larvae do not complete the life cycle and enter body tissues encased in cysts that protect them from most dewormers.

Since mother dogs often pass roundworms to their offspring, puppies should be dewormed when they are very young, starting treatment at about three weeks of age. Many safe dewormers for roundworms are available. The vet will give your

dog one to three doses at first, which will kill the adult worms. Follow-up doses will kill new worms that weren't fully developed when the first doses were given. Most heartworm preventives also protect against roundworms. If you unwisely choose not to put your dog on monthly heartworm protection, he should be dewormed monthly for roundworms.

Tapeworm

Generally reaching about 28 inches (71 cm) long in dogs, tapeworms attach themselves to the intestinal wall and pass visible segments of their body through your dog's feces. Dogs usually contract tapeworm by swallowing an infected flea, but they can also become infected by eating host animals or contaminated feces. These parasites receive their sustenance from your dog, but they are not as serious as other worms. Dewormers can effectively treat tapeworm.

Whipworm

Whipworms are threadlike intestinal parasites that resemble a 2- to 3-inch (5- to 7.5-cm) whip, complete with lash and handle. Transmitted through the ingestion of whipworm eggs, found outdoors or elsewhere in your dog's environment, infections may only cause minor symptoms, such as diarrhea. But in higher numbers, whipworms can cause weight loss and anemia. Dewormers can treat infections, but your dog may require multiple doses. Combination worm preventives are often effective against these parasites.

SPAYING/NEUTERING

Most Poodle owners have a responsibility to spay or neuter their dogs. Not only have most puppies been sold based on this promise, but there are also health and behavioral reasons for these procedures. Of course, the main reason is the control of unwanted puppies.

Spaying removes the uterus and ovaries (though a partial operation in which the ovaries are left behind has gained support in the veterinary community). Spaying can reduce the probability of mammary tumors and prevent uterine cancer, ovarian cysts, false pregnancy, and other issues. Neutering removes the testicles, which reduces your dog's chances of prostate issues, eliminates the risk of testicular cancer, reduces aggression, and makes him less likely to wander.

Traditionally, dogs have been given these operations between six and nine months of age. With new surgical techniques, however, puppies as young as six to eight weeks old can be safely spayed or neutered (a practice sometimes followed in shelters). Early spaying and neutering may prevent behaviors like marking; however, some studies suggest that as far as your dog's health goes, it is better to wait until he is more mature. It is still a controversial issue.

BREED-SPECIFIC DISEASES

Just as people carry genes that cause hereditary disease, so do Poodles. That's the nature of biology. Moreover, some families have a higher incidence of genetic disorders than others do. This is why responsible breeders have potential Poodle parents tested for genetic conditions. Some diseases involve more than one gene or depend on environmental factors to be expressed, which makes understanding and developing predictive tests for them much more difficult.

Because of technological advances, researchers are developing an increasing number of medical tests that allow owners and breeders to screen their dogs for genetic conditions. Screening results for inherited diseases guide breeders in planning matings and inform you about what to watch out for in your dog. Some of the health issues important to Poodles include the following.

ADDISON'S DISEASE

Addison's disease (hypoadrenocorticism) results in inadequate production of adrenal hormones. Primary hypoadrenocorticism concerns the destruction or atrophy of the adrenal cortex and tends to be naturally occurring. Secondary hypoadrenocorticism involves pituitary dysfunction and is often brought on by a sudden withdrawal of steroid drugs used to treat another condition.

Addison's disease, which generally affects female dogs, has been associated with Standard Poodles. Signs vary in their occurrence and intensity, but dogs may experience symptoms including weakness, lethargy, depression, and decreased appetite, among others. The disease can be treated with lifelong administration of an oral hormone replacement.

CHRONIC ACTIVE HEPATITIS

Chronic active hepatitis causes liver inflammation and progressive liver failure. Affected dogs may show decreased appetite, lethargic behavior, and eventually jaundice, diarrhea, vomiting, and other symptoms. Symptoms usually appear around five to seven years of age, when there is significant damage to the liver. Supportive treatment includes medication, dietary changes, and supplementation. Standard Poodles have been associated with this condition.

Standard Poodles have an increased risk of bloat.

ELBOW DYSPLASIA

Elbow dysplasia is the malformation of the elbow due to genetics, trauma, or nutritional factors. More common in larger, faster-growing dogs, this condition causes pain and lameness. Surgery is the best treatment. However, the joints will likely develop degenerative arthritis regardless.

EPILEPSY

According to the American Kennel Club (AKC) Canine Health Foundation (CHF), epilepsy denotes various conditions known for causing "chronic, recurring seizures." Idiopathic (or "primary") epilepsy, which has been associated with Poodles, is classified by an absence of obvious physical causes and is considered genetic. Treatment generally requires ongoing medication but may not be recommended, depending on the frequency and severity of the seizures.

GASTRIC DILATATION-VOLVULUS (GDV) (BLOAT)

Gastric dilatation-volvulus (GDV), more commonly known as "bloat," is a deadly condition in which the stomach becomes filled with gas and twists inside the body, blocking the blood supply to various organs. This condition most commonly affects large, deep-chested dogs and has been associated with dogs eating or drinking too quickly or too much, eating only one meal per day, eating only dry food, and participating in rigorous exercise after a meal.

Signs of GDV include retching, drooling, distressed behavior, and a swollen abdomen. Dogs with GDV should receive emergency veterinary treatment immediately. Veterinarians will try to relieve the pressure in the stomach, and chances of survival are higher with prompt treatment. Standard Poodle owners can help prevent bloat by feeding multiple and smaller meals each day, not using raised dog bowls (which are said to contribute to bloat's occurrence), and keeping dogs from heavy exercise before and after meals.

HEART CONDITIONS

Two heart conditions associated with Poodles are atrial septal defect (ASD) and patent ductus arteriosus (PDA). Both are congenital heart malformations that may shorten your dog's life. Relatively rare in dogs but reported in some Standard Poodles, ASD is a hole in the muscle tissue separating the upper chambers of the heart. When symptoms are present, they may include fatigue, breathing trouble, coughing, and collapse. Heart surgery may be recommended.

PDA is a relatively common canine heart condition associated with Standard, Miniature, and Toy Poodles. When your dog has PDA, the blood vessel that allows blood to bypass the lungs before birth fails to close after birth. This condition may cause breathing trouble, coughing, lethargy, stunted growth, and sometimes congestive heart failure. Surgery may be recommended, and affected dogs should avoid overexertion.

HIP DYSPLASIA

Hip dysplasia involves a malformed hip joint in which the femoral head and the hip socket do not fit properly together. This misalignment and the arthritis it can produce range from mild to severe. Symptoms may include stiffness, pain, unsteady movement, and trouble getting up and climbing stairs, though mild cases may produce no symptoms. Surgery may be recommended, but supportive measures, such as a proper diet, keeping your dog at a healthy weight, mild exercise, and pain medications, can help affected dogs lead normal lives.

HYPOTHYROIDISM

Hypothyroidism involves decreased hormone production in the thyroid and has been associated with Standard Poodles. Clinical signs are most often seen between ages two and five and include hair loss, coat dullness, weight gain, lethargy, and intolerance to the cold. Hypothyroidism is a permanent condition requiring daily doses of thyroid hormone replacement. Dogs with this condition should not be bred.

INHERITED CATARACTS

Generally appearing before age six, inherited cataracts manifest as a clouding of the lens. This may deepen and lead to vision loss or blindness. Inherited cataracts usually affect both eyes, but not always at the same time. Cloudy eyes may have other causes. All dogs who show clouding should be examined by their vet. Surgery may be recommended for advanced cases. Poodles have been associated with this condition, but cataracts are common among most breeds.

JUVENILE RENAL DISEASE (JRD)

Juvenile renal disease (JRD) causes irreversible kidney malformation and has been reported in Standard Poodles. Affected dogs are typically diagnosed by age two and die before age three. Early treatment and proper care, which includes the right diet and supplements, can provide JRD-affected Poodles with longer, more comfortable lives.

LEGG-CALVE-PERTHES DISEASE (LCPD)

Legg-Calve-Perthes disease (LCPD) is a disorder associated with smaller dogs and reported in Miniature and Toy Poodles. Commonly beginning when puppies are between four months and one year old, LCPD involves the deterioration of the femoral head (the "ball" of the hip joint), which can cause stiffness, pain, and lameness. Surgery can successfully treat the condition.

NEONATAL ENCEPHALOPATHY WITH SEIZURES (NEWS)

Neonatal encephalopathy with seizures (NEWS) is a brain disease affecting puppies soon after birth. Signs include weakness, lack of coordination, and dullness. Puppies with NEWS often die within one week. Surviving puppies often experience seizures and generally die before reaching seven weeks old. Standard Poodles have been associated with this condition.

OPTIC NERVE HYPOPLASIA

The uncommon condition optic nerve hypoplasia involves the incomplete development of the optic nerve. Affecting one or both eyes, this condition can result in impaired vision or blindness. It is seen in all three Poodle varieties. Although no treatment is available, dogs with reduced vision can compensate well using their smell and hearing.

PATELLAR LUXATION

Affecting one or both hind legs, patellar luxation is a condition in which the kneecap becomes dislocated. Symptoms include occasional skipping during movement or more frequent carrying of the leg. More commonly affecting Toy and Miniature Poodles than Standards, this condition can be inherited or result from trauma. Treatment methods include surgery or pain medication, depending on the patient. Minor cases may not require treatment.

PROGRESSIVE RETINAL ATROPHY (PRA)

Progressive retinal atrophy (PRA) denotes various conditions involving the retina. Initially affecting a dog's ability to see in the dark, PRA eventually causes dogs to lose their daytime vision and become blind. Miniature and Toy Poodles have been known to carry the recessive progressive-rod-cone-degeneration (PRDC) PRA gene. Though they are less often associated with PRA, some Standard Poodles have shown a different form of the condition.

SEBACEOUS ADENITIS (SA)

Sebaceous adenitis (SA) is an inherited skin disease in which the sebaceous glands, responsible for producing a skin-and-hair lubricant called "sebum," become inflamed. Often leading to progressive hair loss, SA an develop when your dog is as young as a year old or have its onset delayed longer than a decade. Standard Poodles represent the majority of Poodle cases.

VON WILLEBRAND DISEASE (VWD)

Von Willebrand disease (vWD) is the deficiency or dysfunction of von Willebrand factor, a glycoprotein that supports blood clotting. vWD comes in three types, the first being the most common and mildest and the others being more serious. All types can cause excessive bleeding, which requires veterinary attention, but the likelihood is higher with types 2 and 3. Standard Poodles have been associated with this condition.

GENERAL HEALTH ISSUES

Beyond the more breed-specific conditions described above, your Poodle may experience other issues that are common to all breeds. Whether they suffer from allergies or infections, dogs succumb to the same everyday health problems that we do. These can be serious, lifelong conditions or minor episodes in an otherwise healthy life.

ALLERGIES

Allergies are abnormal reactions to food or medicine, something inhaled (grasses, molds, pollens), fleas or other biting insects, or something else in your dog's environment. The irritant, or "allergen," triggers the dog's immune system to react. Symptoms of allergies include excessive scratching or licking, hives, sneezing, vomiting, diarrhea, and an affected temperament. Poodles are especially subject to inhaled and contact allergies.

Most allergies can be handled by limiting exposure to the allergen, whether it be fleas, pollen (cleaning your dog's coat more frequently during allergy season to reduce itching), or certain kinds of food. Symptoms themselves can be relieved with medications, including antihistamines and medicated baths. Cortisone may be recommended for more persistent cases.

CANCER

Cancer affects many dogs. According to a University of Georgia College of Veterinary Medicine study investigating Veterinary Medical Database (VMDB) records, cancer was the leading cause of death in North American dogs over the age of two from 1984 to 2004, and it caused death more commonly in larger breeds. Poodles have a higher incidence of breast tumors than most breeds.

Cancer involves the uncontrolled, invasive growth of cells in one or various parts of the body. Symptoms include lumps, persistent sores, lethargy, weight loss, and loss of appetite, among others. Treatment methods are similar to those for humans and include surgery, radiation, and chemotherapy. Supportive treatment can provide comfort to affected dogs.

EAR INFECTIONS

Ear infections are mundane but potentially serious issues. Common causes include dampness, the presence of foreign material, and ear mites. Overzealous plucking of hair from the ear canal may also cause infection. Common symptoms include head shaking or titling, scratching, redness, swelling, discharge, and odor. Dogs with inner ear infections may appear dizzy.

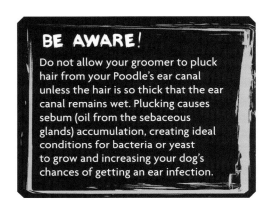

BE AWARE!

Do not allow your groomer to pluck hair from your Poodle's ear canal unless the hair is so thick that the ear canal remains wet. Plucking causes sebum (oil from the sebaceous glands) accumulation, creating ideal conditions for bacteria or yeast to grow and increasing your dog's chances of getting an ear infection.

Ear infections require prompt veterinary attention. Vets generally perform a professional cleaning and prescribe ear medicine accompanied by home cleaning. Without veterinary care, infections may become more serious and lead to hearing loss, meningitis, or other issues.

EYE PROBLEMS

Eye problems can crop up in dogs just like they can in people. Poodles have predilections to certain eye conditions, but many issues are shared by dogs of all breeds. Common ones include conjunctivitis (or "pink eye"), cataracts (common to Poodles, but most breeds are susceptible), glaucoma (increased pressure in the eye), and keratoconjunctivitis sicca (known as "dry eye").

Common symptoms of eye problems include discharge, discoloration, clouding, squinting, eye, face, or head rubbing, and increased tearing or blinking. Some eye conditions can lead to vision loss or blindness, so dogs showing symptoms should be seen by a veterinarian promptly.

ALTERNATIVE THERAPIES

The American Holistic Veterinary Medical Association (AHVMA) describes the holistic approach as considering all aspects of the animal's life and using a combination of conventional and alternative approaches to treat disease.

Commonly thought to be an eye infection in Poodles, "Poodle eye" refers to the facial staining that can result from tearing. Also known as tearstaining, this is primarily a cosmetic issue, but dogs with tearstains should be examined by the vet. If there is no medical cause, then after your Poodle's hair is clipped close to his face, tearstains can be addressed with daily cleaning to decrease the discoloration.

Holistic practitioners examine your Poodle's environment, medical history, and relationship with you to develop a treatment program from the range of therapies available for healing. They believe that lasting recovery can be provided by addressing the root causes of illness, which may lie between layers of symptoms and other causes. Among the methods of therapy used by holistic veterinarians are acupuncture, chiropractic, herbal, homeopathy, and physical therapy.

ACUPUNCTURE

Similar to human acupuncture, veterinary acupuncture involves using needles to access key points along the body to provide relief and healing. According to the International Veterinary Acupuncture Society (IVAS), practitioners in China have performed veterinary acupuncture for millennia. Veterinary acupuncture addresses many conditions, including those affecting various body systems, such as the musculoskeletal, respiratory, gastrointestinal, and reproductive systems.

CHIROPRACTIC

Another treatment method that has become increasingly popular with people, chiropractic involves the relationship between the spinal cord and the nervous system. Small adjustments made to the spine by a veterinary chiropractor are said to restore nerve communication that had previously been blocked. Restoring proper spinal alignment is said to benefit dogs physically, provide relief to dogs with arthritis and other conditions, and strengthen the immune system.

HERBAL

Herbal medicine practitioners use herbs and extracts from plants to help support the healing process. According to the AHVMA, herbal medicine can help your pets physically, emotionally, and mentally. Check with your veterinarian before giving your dog herbal medicine, as these medicines can have strong physical effects that pet owners may not anticipate.

HOMEOPATHY

Based on the idea that a small amount of a toxic substance can be a cure, homeopathy strives to treat the vibrational root of disease (according to the AHVMA, "the deepest constitutional causes of illness") with remedies made from elements as diverse as bacteria, plants, and drugs. As with herbal medicine, consult your veterinarian before giving your dog homeopathic remedies.

PHYSICAL THERAPY

Just like people, dogs can benefit from physical therapy. Canine physical therapy is a rapidly growing field that utilizes the same methods and even equipment used for human beings. Techniques include massage, thermo- and cryotherapy, passive range-of-motion exercises, balance exercises, coordination exercises, electrical stimulation, and hydrotherapy. (The underwater treadmills come equipped with filters to remove dog hair.)

Many dog owners swear by the effectiveness of Tellington TTouch, a physical therapy technique designed to reduce stress and help animals gain greater focus. It consists of circular touches, lifts, and light strokes to the skin, especially around the ears, which produce a calming effect many dog owners can attest to.

FIRST AID

Dogs are bound to have adventures, and sometimes those adventures require first aid. Canine first aid is a large topic, but basically, you're going to want to keep your dog calm, carefully stop any bleeding, and call your veterinarian for help.

Having a first-aid kit can be helpful. Conduct research online to plan your canine first-aid kit, which should include first-aid items, instructions on responding to emergency situations, addresses and phone numbers for your veterinarian and your local emergency veterinary clinic, and the phone number for ASPCA Animal Poison Control (888-426-4435).

Below are some general guidelines for common problems dog owners should prevent, if possible: frostbite, heatstroke, and poisoning. These are serious problems, but knowing how to respond can save your Poodle's life. Keep your veterinarian's phone number and the number for a nearby emergency animal clinic available at all times.

FROSTBITE

Frostbite is the actual freezing of tissue, usually seen in the tail, ears, and feet. The skin will appear blue or very white. The frozen tissue must not be rubbed or allowed to refreeze after thawing. If your Poodle gets frostbite, call your veterinarian or an emergency clinic immediately and ask for instructions. Your vet should examine the damage when possible and determine whether tissue needs surgical removal.

Frostbite can be avoided by giving your dog warm clothing to wear when it's cold outside and not staying outside with him for too long.

HEATSTROKE

With their fur coats and ineffective cooling mechanisms (which are limited to panting and sweating through their foot pads), dogs overheat more easily than people do. When their body temperature rises to 104°F (40°C), they can experience heatstroke, a deadly condition that needs immediate treatment. Symptoms of heatstroke include heavy panting, trouble breathing, a bright-red tongue, thickened saliva, vomiting, and bloody diarrhea. This condition eventually causes shock, collapse, seizures, and death.

Overheating can occur in many situations. Dogs left inside parked cars (where temperatures can rise by almost 30°F [16.5°C] in 20 minutes, even when it's only 70°F [21°C] outside) overheat surprisingly quickly. Therefore, you should never leave your dog in the car. Other situations that can cause heatstroke are rigorous exercise (or confinement without shade and water) on hot days, being confined to concrete or asphalt, and being muzzled or confined underneath a hair dryer. Fevers and seizures can also result in heatstroke.

If your dog shows signs of heatstroke, remove him promptly from the heat and take a rectal temperature reading (checking again every 10 minutes). If his temperature is above 104°F (40°C), start running cool water over his body (not

Dogs depend on panting for cooling because they don't sweat effectively.

cold water, which can cause further harm) in the bathtub and massaging his legs. Continue cooling him, supplementing with a cold pack applied to his head, until his temperature falls below 103°F (39.5°C). Once it does, stop cooling and dry. Further cooling may induce hypothermia and shock. Take him to a veterinarian immediately. Complications from heatstroke can occur hours or days later.

POISONING

Many dogs eat first and ask questions later. When they ingest things like medicine, dead animals, household cleaners, antifreeze, certain foods ("What to Feed Your Poodle," Chapter 4), or other hazardous substances from a host of unimagined sources available to the curious dog, they can be poisoned. In many cases, the cause of the poisoning is never discovered.

Should you think your dog has been poisoned, grab the available evidence (medicine bottles, food wrappers, etc.) and call your veterinarian, the nearest emergency veterinary clinic, or ASPCA Animal Poison Control at 888-426-4435 (a consultation fee may apply). Tell them as much as you can about the ingested substance and follow their instructions, which may involve bringing your dog to the clinic as soon as possible. Never induce vomiting without professional approval, because some poisons cause further damage when regurgitated.

SENIOR DOGS

Aging is breed-specific and related to your dog's size. Standard Poodles usually have shorter life spans than their smaller counterparts. Standards, who are seniors at age 9 or 10, are considered old at 12 years and sometimes reach age 14. Minis, seniors around age 12, are truly elderly at 15 or 16. Toys live the longest. Senior status for Toy Poodles begins at age 13, and they are old at 18 or 19.

Some physical indications that your dog is aging include grayness around his muzzle, loss of muscle tone and strength (especially in the legs), some arthritis or stiffness, reduction in hearing and vision, and perhaps a decrease in energy. Additional signs include changes in skin and coat, including the appearance of fatty tumors called lipomas, which are usually not harmful.

Behavioral changes often result from physical changes that are occurring. Older dogs do not adjust well to changes in their routine, being hurried, being boarded in a kennel, or heat and cold. Sometimes they experience confusion and seem to be lost. Areas of your dog's body may hurt when they are touched, causing him to react to petting in an aggressive manner. Chewing may become more difficult. There may be increased thirst and house soiling. Older dogs need more time to change gears—from sleep to waking, from lying down to standing, from walking to the potty stop. Everything goes at a slower pace, and sleep is more important.

Senior dogs need special care to help accommodate their changing physical condition.

SENIOR DOG HEALTH

A twice-annual checkup should be done for every dog more than seven years old to prevent premature aging. Although there are diseases seen more often in seniors, such as arthritis and canine cognitive dysfunction (CCD), most senior illnesses aren't necessarily *different* than those seen at other ages. What is different is the ability of the body to cope with the changes illness causes. In addition, a fragile body increases the chance that an illness—or the therapy for that illness—will also cause secondary problems.

With any serious chronic conditions affecting your senior Poodle, you should continually discuss with your veterinarian the trade-offs between various types of therapy and your Poodle's quality of life. With many medications and therapies, there are limits to what they can accomplish. Often, the most helpful approach is to change what can be changed and to adapt to the rest of the limitations caused by the chronic disease.

CARING FOR YOUR SENIOR DOG

Caring for older dogs is about minimizing physical and emotional stress and meeting the special needs of these elder statesmen. One of the most important ways to keep your senior healthy is to keep him stimulated mentally and physically. Walking is important exercise, and swimming is excellent because it allows him to use his entire body without putting pressure on his joints. However, keep in mind that your Poodle will be less able to regulate his body temperature and will become tired and cold sooner. You can take more frequent but shorter walks to help accommodate Poodles who are slowing down, especially on cold days.

You may need to install nonskid treads on stairs or area rugs in places where your senior Poodle must walk as part of his everyday life. Especially for arthritis pain, seek to eliminate the use of stairs in your daily routine, if possible. When this is not possible, alternatives include carrying your dog up and down or using ramps, both of which can also help with getting into the car. Keeping your Poodle's nails short will help keep slipping to a minimum, as will frequently clipping the hair on his feet.

Decreased vision and hearing present other challenges. Dogs with hearing loss may ignore commands when you are together unless you use hand signals. Another challenge is awakening them. Don't touch them to wake them up. Instead, awaken them by stamping your foot on the floor nearby. The vibrations will get your dog's attention. Changes in vision can be helped by blocking off stairways with a gate to prevent an accidental tumble.

Playing games indoors, especially during the winter, can keep your senior dog mentally sharp. "Find it" is a favorite indoor game. First place your dog in a *sit-stay* and show him the ball or toy you're going to hide. Then creep away and hide the object. Come back to your dog. Tap him on the chest to release him and say, "Find it." Make it easy for him to find the object the first few times. Then gradually increase the difficulty. Fifteen minutes of "find it" will make your dog feel needed, joyful, stimulated. And it will give him something to dream about in his next nap.

TRAINING
YOUR POODLE

Training improves your communication with your Poodle. Through working and having fun together, your relationship will deepen, and as you learn together, you will develop the tools and mutual understanding necessary for getting over the tricky and awkward moments that you share. Training also allows you to better understand each other's expectations, whether you're going for walks, relaxing at home, visiting the groomer (who may be you!), going on vacation, meeting new friends, or sharing other experiences with your best friend.

Of the many books, television shows, and even podcasts on training, much that is popular is not very effective. That's because, as with commitments like weight loss, people want to believe that training can be accomplished in two weeks if you have the magic technique. Though training can change your Poodle's life, things won't shift overnight. Good results require consistent practice.

POSITIVE TRAINING

Dog training involves arenas like socialization, household manners, and responding to different commands. For training to work, it is important that you learn how to reward the behavior you want from your dog and stop rewarding behavior you don't want. Positive training shows your dog what to do rather than admonishing him for doing something else.

Training helps you communicate more clearly with your Poodle.

Some people mistakenly give their dogs what they want to stop undesirable behavior. When you let your dog out of the crate when he barks to be free, you're training him to bark. Domination-based training methods, meanwhile, damage your dog–owner relationship and provide ineffective education. They produce aggressive, fearful dogs and often don't show them what you want them to do. Physical force (yelling, rolling, pushing, spanking) has no place in positive training.

Positive training is about having your Poodle willingly take action and then giving him praise, food, or other rewards in exchange. When your dog behaves undesirably, positive training involves removing something he wants to show him that the behavior doesn't get him what he's looking for. This approach makes it easy for him to cooperate and creates positive associations with doing so. The methods described here are positive, reward-based methods. Punishment will never get you what you want from your Poodle.

SOCIALIZATION

The process of socialization is the gradual exposure of your dog to aspects of everyday life. These might include other dogs and pets, different people (especially kids), noisy environments, new smells, and other unfamiliar experiences. When your dog is well socialized, he understands how he is supposed to behave wherever he goes. He feels comfortable around new people and is accustomed to everyday sights and sounds.

HOW TO SOCIALIZE YOUR POODLE

Good breeders socialize their puppies for the first eight weeks of their lives, showing them things like television, visitors, and kids. They expose them to different toys, places to wander around the house, smooth floors, cushy carpets. If you have a puppy, he should already have developed relationships with littermates and gotten a taste of the household experience.

At eight weeks of age, puppies are too young for outdoor walks and haven't completed the proper immunizations for them. However, until your puppy is ready for those big adventures through the neighborhood, you can take him to trusted friends' homes and introduce him to immunized dogs and cats.

Socialization should always feel safe for your dog. Between 8 and 12 weeks of age, puppies remember all of their frightening experiences, and even older dogs can be traumatized by upsetting situations. When starting out, it is important that you do not force your Poodle to face his fears. His days should be packed with meeting kind, gentle people, riding in the car, socializing with other dogs (both puppies and adults), and beginner training sessions. If he becomes fearful, distract him with a toy. Let him retreat. Don't make him interact—entice him to interact. You'll forever appreciate your caution during your Poodle's early socialization period.

As your Poodle gets older, socialization should expand outward. You can venture outside with him, meet new friends (or pass them by on the sidewalk), hear new sounds. You and your Poodle can watch people ride bicycles. Observe neighborhood birds and squirrels.

Socialization should expand even more. When you only groom, feed, cuddle, housetrain, and walk your Poodle, that's the extent of his universe. He doesn't know how to adapt to different locations, crowds, being crated, and so forth. In other words, without expanding your Poodle's boundaries, you're limiting his development. Well-socialized dogs are adaptable. Dogs who are not widely socialized may not be. Socialization is something that we humans are responsible for providing to man's best friend.

CRATE TRAINING

Crates are gifts both to dogs and to their owners. They provide protection, privacy, comfort, and structure. When used correctly, they hasten housetraining and make your puppy more secure. Crate-trained dogs regard their crates as dens and enjoy spending quiet time there. Crates protect dogs from raucous kids, large electricians stamping around the house and leaving the door open and other household dangers.

Crates are also convenient devices to have when you travel, during an emergency, or when you need to take your dog safely to the vet. You can briefly "stash" your Poodle when you're, say, cooking dinner, taking a bath, or trying to get the leaky toilet under control.

The crate should be located in a quiet but not isolated part of the house. It should be large enough for your dog to stand and turn around in but not big enough to be

PUPPY POINTER

Puppies raised with chickens between 8 and 12 weeks of age don't chase or attack them. In the same way, puppies raised with cats, ferrets, parrots, gerbils, or goats consider those animals normal parts of their household. If you don't have children but plan to add to your family, be sure to expose your puppy to the sights, sounds, and smells of small children. Dogs not accustomed to children are often made nervous by their, shrill voices and unpredictable movements.

unwieldy, for him to eliminate in one side and sleep on the other, or to give him a feeling of being lost. It should be comfortably outfitted with a soft crate pad and a chew toy or two for entertainment.

The crate should never be used to punish your dog or imprison him for hours on end while you are off skiing for the day. Your Poodle should consider this space his den, his sanctuary. Always maintain positive associations with the crate so that he remains comfortable there and accepts being crated when you need him to be.

HOW TO CRATE TRAIN YOUR POODLE

When you crate train, keep in mind that the crate is a tool for you and a safe haven of pleasure for your dog. When you're starting out, consider placing multiple crates around the house. Put one in the kitchen or family room (if you don't have an exercise pen there), one in the room where you sleep, and one in the car. As with any crate, furnish each with a crate pad. During training, keep the crate doors fastened open so that they won't hit and frighten your Poodle.

Crate training is all about getting your dog comfortable with being in the crate. Introduce him to the crate with short practice sessions during the day. Decide on a universal command, usually something original like "Crate!" (but it can be "Jabberwocky!" for all the dog cares), and say it whenever your Poodle enters the crate.

Getting him inside is another matter. Toss a chew treat into the crate to get him interested. If he's reluctant, progress more slowly. Give him a treat when he approaches the crate and inspects it. When he does follow the treat inside, say your command, hang out by the crate, and praise him while he eats. Keep the door open so that he doesn't associate the crate with punishment. When your dog is more comfortable, do the same routine, but quietly shut the door. Make sure to stay close-by. Gradually you can increase the time he spends inside.

One good way to upgrade your training is to feed meals in the crate. When your dog has gotten comfortable with the shorter excursions, start placing his food bowl all the way in the back of the crate. Should he hesitate, place it as far in as he willingly goes and move the bowl back each day. Once he is eating comfortably, close the door while he eats and open it as soon as he is finished. With each feeding, leave the door closed longer, until he's in the crate 10 minutes after eating.

After a while, leave for short periods while he's in the crate. Don't make a big fuss when you return. Condition him for longer periods as he gets more comfortable. If your Poodle whines, wait until he is quiet to release him from the crate. Otherwise, you're training him to whine when he wants to get out. (The exception is when he's whining to go potty at night. In this case, calmly take him out as soon as he starts making noise.) Especially when housetraining, take him to his potty spot whenever you release him from the crate.

Crating at Night

As mentioned above, another useful practice routine is crating your Poodle when you go to sleep. By keeping a crate next to your bed, not only can you keep each other company, but you can also hear him more easily if he whines to go out at night. During housetraining—at least if you have a puppy—this will be a nightly occurrence.

Though you should get your puppy used to the crate before using it during the day so that you develop good associations, putting your Poodle in the crate at night should begin as soon as you bring him home. This is where crate training goes hand in hand with housetraining.

CRATING TIME LIMITS

Except for crating your dog at night during housetraining and the early stages of crate training, you shouldn't keep him in a crate for more than a couple of hours at a time without a break. Dogs need to exercise their minds and bodies. If you must be away for a good part of the day and don't trust your dog to stay out of trouble, consider dog daycare or a reliable dog walker. You should get someone to let him out in the afternoon anyway if he's a puppy. During their first six months, puppies should not be expected to hold their bladders for longer than a few hours.

HOUSETRAINING

When your Poodle is housetrained, he will know not to potty in the house and will ask you to take him outside when he needs to go. Normally, a puppy knows not to potty where he sleeps by eight weeks, but teaching him where he should eliminate requires consistency and determination.

Crates provide invaluable assistance while you housetrain your puppy.

GETTING STARTED

Creating a schedule is your first step to effective housetraining. Schedule a potty break for each of the following times: when you get up in the morning, after every meal, between meals (based on your dog's age; see below), and before you go to bed. Record the time of day whenever he successfully eliminates (including indoor accidents) and update your schedule accordingly.

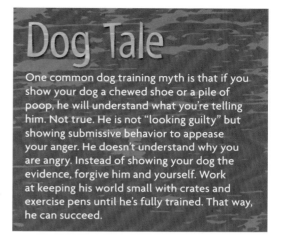

Dog Tale

One common dog training myth is that if you show your dog a chewed shoe or a pile of poop, he will understand what you're telling him. Not true. He is not "looking guilty" but showing submissive behavior to appease your anger. He doesn't understand why you are angry. Instead of showing your dog the evidence, forgive him and yourself. Work at keeping his world small with crates and exercise pens until he's fully trained. That way, he can succeed.

Updates may reflect commonly occurring accidents, your Poodle growing up, or other factors.

Until he's about six months old, your puppy's age in months approximately equals how many hours he can go without a potty break. So if he's two months old, he should go out once every two hours. He may also need to go after playing, waking up from a nap, and getting excited. These factors may contribute to your daily schedule. Once you have your schedule, follow it, bringing your Poodle out whenever he's supposed to go.

You should also learn the signals that your dog uses to show you he needs to potty. Even while following a schedule, your dog may need to potty throughout the day, and there are various ways you can tell. Common ones include spinning in circles, sniffing around, panting, and whining. Your dog may have other signals, too. Jot down notes about his behavior, especially preceding an accident, and watch for these patterns during housetraining. Bring him out promptly whenever you see his signals. Otherwise, he may slacken his signals and start going inside.

HOW TO HOUSETRAIN YOUR POODLE

With your basic schedule established, housetraining can be a simple process. Consistency is the key. Being inconsistent and ignoring your Poodle's signals can slow down your progress. Every time your dog eliminates in the house without your intervention (see below section on interrupting indoor events) contributes to the pattern of going inside. However, every time you bring him outside for a successful potty break, you're establishing good patterns. When your dog is housetrained and gives signals with confidence, you will be glad you were so committed.

The Everyday Routine

When you bring your Poodle outside to go potty, bring him to the same place every time. Having this consistent potty place will show him where to potty and helps things move more efficiently. Wait there silently with him on leash until he eliminates. When he starts to go, say, "Potty," or another command word of your choosing. When he's done, praise him and give him a treat. If he doesn't go within 5 minutes, crate him for 15 minutes and then try again.

Housetraining means following the schedule, watching for signals. If you are not a compulsive schedule follower, program alarms on your phone to remind you when your Poodle needs to go. Otherwise, he will have been walking back and forth, whining, which you will not have noticed because you were absorbed in your work. Finally, he will pee indoors because his little bladder couldn't hold it any longer.

Scheduling potty breaks makes your Poodle's housetraining routine much easier.

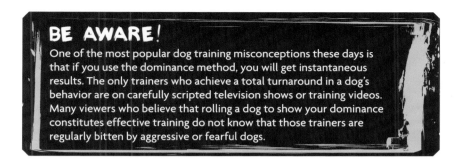

Workday and Night

Workdays and nighttime are often the most stressful periods for housetraining, but they can be simple enough. During the day, if you're at work and can't come home for lunch, have a friend or professional dog walker let your Poodle out at least once, if not two or three times. When your Poodle is housetrained and old enough to wait until you get home, make sure you leave work on time and bring him out as soon as you get back (or schedule someone to be there for you).

Every night, 30 minutes before bedtime, put away your Poodle's water bowl. Before you crate him for the night, bring him to his potty spot. Remember, you're following the potty protocol every single time. Whenever he wakes you up at night, bring him out again. Crate him when you come back inside. When you wake up in the morning, bring him out for his morning potty break.

Interrupting an Indoor Event

When you see your puppy eliminate indoors, take advantage of the situation to strengthen his housetraining. Cry out, "Uh-oh!" sharply. Most pups will stop urinating to stare at you and wonder what the fuss is all about. Scoop him up in your arms and speed him to the appropriate spot outside. Don't scold him; yelling at him when he's eliminating inside will just make him hide next time he does it. Yelling at him after he eliminates will just scare him, because he won't know what you're talking about, even if you're pointing to the mess.

You're lucky if you catch him going inside, because you can then show him the proper potty place and reinforce the positive message. Poodles are smart dogs and usually get the message pretty quickly. However, Toy Poodles (and this is true of all toy breeds) need more patience in this regard. Partly because of their tiny bladders, housetraining is more of an ordeal for them.

If your dog has soiled the area, clean it thoroughly with soap and water and then with a product designed for urine removal. Removing the smell will help prevent him from going there again. Note when the accident occurred or when you found the mess for your potty training schedule.

BASIC OBEDIENCE COMMANDS

Basic obedience commands serve various functions. Training them strengthens your Poodle–human relationship, improves your communication, and gives you ways to distract your dog from unwanted behavior. With consistent practice and positive training, your dog will walk nicely on leash, come back when you call him, and become your closest companion.

Practicing positive reinforcement will help you keep your Poodle on the right track. He is sure to respond to the promise of a reward, which can be anything he likes: a treat, a ball or squeaky toy, words of praise, or an ear scratch. Because so many dogs love them, treats are recommended in the following training instructions. Keep healthy treats in your pocket or invest in a "bait sack," because you will be training throughout your Poodle's daily schedule.

TRAINING GUIDELINES

Deliver each training command when your Poodle performs the behavior so that he associates the command with the action. Then mark each behavior upon completion (either by clicking your clicker once or firmly saying, "Yes") and reward your dog. Keep your vocal tone consistent when giving command words and your verbal marker. **Note:** The clicker makes marking each behavior easy because the sound remains consistent and won't be confused with the command words.

Keep practice sessions short enough that your dog remains engaged. Fifteen minutes each day should be sufficient, spread out

Sit is an easy command to teach, so it's a good one to start with.

over two or three practice sessions. After many successful repetitions you can start alternating treats with praise so that your dog knows that he won't always receive food for the command and so that he won't eat too many snacks.

Always wait until your Poodle is confidently trained to say the command outside of a training session, and only say the command once each time. If he doesn't perform the requested behavior, ignore him until he does. Then give him lots of praise. If he still doesn't respond, continue basic training before trying again. Otherwise, you might teach him to ignore you.

SIT

The *sit* is perfect as a distraction from what your dog is doing. In addition, it's an easy command to teach, so it's a good one to start with. Once you train *sit*, you can practice throughout the day, having your Poodle sit before eating, going outside for a walk, or greeting guests. This will help you establish a steady foundation for cooperation with your dog.

How to Train *Sit*
Have your treats ready and follow these steps to train your dog to sit.
1. Hold a treat just above your Poodle's head.
2. When he reaches up, his head will rise and his bottom will drop.
3. Say, "Sit," as he sits down. Mark the behavior and treat.

   Repeat the exercise many times each day. While you might want to start in a quiet environment to reduce the amount of distractions, gradually introduce more distracting environments to your training sessions to help your dog more confidently learn the behavior.

COME

While *sit* is the most basic command, *come* may be the most important. When your Poodle knows how to come back to you, you can get him to return to you should he get loose outside, chew something that could hurt him, or head somewhere you don't want him to go. Telling your dog to stop is often too vague, but calling him back to you can get the same results.

How to Train *Come*
You can start training *come* by simply praising your puppy every time he comes to you—even if you haven't called him. When he's ready for more formal training, you can continue the process with training sessions from a close distance, perhaps inside the exercise pen.

1. Act engaging, kneeling or sitting down and clapping your hands.
2. When he comes, happily but firmly say, "[Poodle's name], come!"
3. When your Poodle gets there, mark the behavior. Give him a treat.

Eventually, you can start to practice outside, perhaps after potty breaks, with your Poodle on the leash. Add more distraction and distance as time goes on. With *come*, adding distractions is especially important so that your Poodle responds when you need him to. However, even well-trained dogs might not

Food is a great reward when you are training your Poodle.

return to you when they're heavily distracted. The biggest rule about *come* is to never punish your dog for responding to the command—no matter what he's done. Maintain positive associations with him coming back to you.

DOWN

When you use *down*, you can help your dog relax. This command brings him a sense of grounding after whatever he has been doing. *Down* can be helpful when removing his leash after a walk or during other situations wherein you want him to take a breather.

How to Train *Down*

Start training *down* with your Poodle leashed in a quiet environment.
1. Ask your Poodle to sit.
2. Once he sits, lure him down with the treat between your fingers.
3. Say, "Down," while he's dropping down.
4. When he's lying down, mark the behavior.
5. Give him the treat.

As with the other commands, gradually practice *down* in more distracting environments until he confidently performs the behavior wherever he goes.

STAY

Stay helps your dog complete his other commands more effectively. When you ask him to stay, you're asking him to remain motionless until you release him. Use *stay* to keep your Poodle lying down during dinner or while you bring groceries across the room. *Stay* can be challenging because it's about not moving, but with continuous practice and rewards throughout your lives together, this command can remain fresh in your Poodle's mind.

How to Train *Stay*

1. Have your Poodle leashed and seated beside you.
2. With one hand holding the leash, raise the other palm toward your dog's face, ending before his nose. Say, "Stay."
3. Step backward once. After one full second, mark the behavior.
4. Give your release word (something you rarely say, such as "release").
5. Give your dog a treat.

After three practice sessions, play around with your Poodle. Then practice some more. When your Poodle knows the command, practice before dinner, making him sit and stay while you put the empty bowl down. When he goes for it, pick it back up and repeat the process. When your Poodle gets the idea and stays while the bowl is on the ground, mark the behavior, give your release word, and fill the bowl. Practicing before meals reinforces this command quickly.

HEEL (WALK NICELY ON LEASH)

Walking nicely on leash may be the most useful training your Poodle receives. While other commands have effective functions, training *heel* makes every walk with your Poodle more relaxing, even without using the command. Walking nicely on leash shows how these training sessions can cultivate wordless cooperation with your dog, one of their most rewarding and impressive benefits. Moreover, when your dog is trained to walk nicely, he'll be more likely to do so with family members, professional trainers, and professional dog walkers too.

How to Train *Heel*

Begin your *heel* training in the hallway or another quiet place without distractions.

1. With your Poodle wearing his regular collar, put on his regular leash.

Your Poodle should learn to walk nicely on leash so that your life together is pleasant.

2. Begin with him standing on your left side.
3. Walk forward briskly so that he knows which direction you're going.
4. Keep walking as long as your Poodle is even with your feet.
5. Say, "Heel," while he's walking beside you.
6. When he sprints ahead, stop. Wait for him to return and sit down.
7. When he does, mark the behavior and give him a treat.
8. Begin walking again Say, "Heel," while he walks beside you.
9. When he sprints ahead, stop. Wait for him to return and sit down.
10. When he does, mark the behavior and give him a treat.

   You get the idea, and so will your Poodle. Repeat the process until the end of your practice session. Your progress may seem slow, but this stopping and starting teaches your dog that you're not going to keep walking unless he stays beside you throughout your journey.

HOW TO FIND A PROFESSIONAL TRAINER

The professional trainer is a guide to your dog's mind. The best professional trainers help you and your Poodle have fun while you achieve obedience goals, learn new commands, and improve your communication. Trainers can also help you remember that your dog is not a human being in a Poodle suit. He doesn't deliberately ignore you or plot against you. Dogs remember things, but they don't worry about the past or plan for the future.

POODLE

106

You can arrange for private sessions or training classes. For your Poodle, the interaction with other dogs and people is important. Many trainers offer different classes for different ages and sizes of dogs as well as supervised playgroups to help socialize them. Whatever the scenario, your trainer will help you strengthen your relationship with and receive what you want from your Poodle.

Good trainers are accredited and experienced. They belong to professional organizations and attend many professional meetings and continuing-education classes, continually improving their skills. They teach lots of classes and private clients. Good trainers will tell you that they learn something new from every dog they meet. Good trainers use positive training methods.

Finding the right trainer takes a few telephone calls and a bit of interviewing. Your breeder and veterinarian should be good sources of information about local trainers who get good reviews. In addition, professional dog training organizations often provide member directories to help you find trainers in your area. Some popular organizations include the Association of Professional Dog Trainers (APDT), the Certification Council for Professional Dog Trainers (CCPDT), and the National Association of Dog Obedience Instructors (NADOI). Remember that while trainers offer an important service, classes should also be fun for you and your Poodle. If you don't feel comfortable with your trainer, keep looking.

Good trainers should be accredited, experienced, and devoted to positive training.

CHAPTER 8

SOLVING PROBLEMS
WITH YOUR POODLE

We recognize problem behaviors when we see them ("Barry's been barking for hours. That's a problem"), but what are they, really? Essentially, a problem behavior is anything your dog does that differs from your expectations of how he should behave when he does it. Problem behaviors are contextual, not absolute.

Dogs often follow instincts that clash with their social environment. What they're doing is then considered inappropriate. Sometimes behaviors, say, chewing, that are contextually welcome coupled with certain variables, like chew toys and the couch, become contextually unwelcome with others, like shoes and your bedroom. Your Poodle may have no idea what is wrong with certain actions, but because he lives with people, some behaviors become problem behaviors.

WHAT CAUSES PROBLEM BEHAVIORS?

While problem behaviors have many causes, four basic reasons often apply.

1. **Excess energy:** Professional dog trainers have a saying: "A tired dog is a good dog." Most dogs don't get enough physical or mental stimulation, and their excess energy often funnels into barking, chewing, and other problem behaviors.
2. **Inadequate training:** Oftentimes, dogs have not been trained to behave otherwise. They are just following their instincts, and unfortunately, their instincts have been considered inappropriate by their human friends.
3. **Miscommunication:** Human beings are not nearly as good at reading dog body language as dogs are at reading ours. Our nonverbal language often sends mixed messages about what our dogs should be doing.
4. **Misunderstanding:** Humans often read into their dog's actions an intent that isn't there, which can cause them to misunderstand the reason for their dog's behavior and miss what their dog is trying to tell them.

Unraveling most problem behaviors requires first meeting your dog's needs, then understanding what causes him to "misbehave," and then offering consistent, firm, loving guidance so that your dog learns when his behavior is appropriate and when it's not.

As explained in the last chapter, physical force and punishment will not resolve unwanted behaviors from your dog and will actually make problems worse, especially problem behaviors rooted in aggression or fear. They will also damage your dog–owner relationship.

More persistent problem behaviors may require guidance from a professional dog trainer or behaviorist. See "When to Seek Professional Help" at the end of this chapter if your Poodle's problem behaviors have become dangerous or overwhelming. Sometimes problem behaviors indicate health issues, so discuss ongoing situations with your veterinarian.

BARKING (EXCESSIVE)

Most dogs like to bark. They do it to call your attention to robbers, to let you know they wish to exit the house, to demand dinner, to make you notice the Yorkie across the street, or because they feel like it. No one minds a warning bark or two, but when the barking becomes incessant, a major problem can develop. Not between you and the dog, necessarily, but between you and the neighbors. In fact, excessive barking is one the main reasons dogs are given away. (Standard Poodles are perhaps less apt to bark than many other breeds, however.)

HOW TO SOLVE EXCESSIVE BARKING

Possible causes for excessive and inappropriate barking are legion. Your Poodle may have a legitimate reason for barking that you're not responding to, he may have been rewarded in the past for barking, or he may not have gotten enough exercise today. To help resolve this problem, you should first make sure you're meeting your Poodle's needs and then work from there.

Meeting Your Poodle's Needs

Easily distracted people may find their dogs barking at them for various reasons throughout the day. They may not have taken their Poodle out to the bathroom in a while or given him dinner at his appointed time. Their dog may feel too cold, too hot, or ready for them to groom his matted coat. These are legitimate reasons

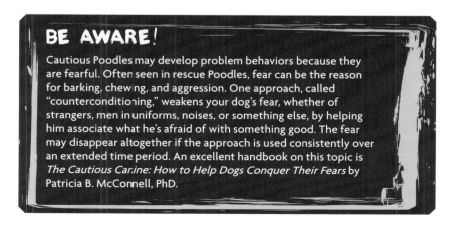

BE AWARE!

Cautious Poodles may develop problem behaviors because they are fearful. Often seen in rescue Poodles, fear can be the reason for barking, chewing, and aggression. One approach, called "counterconditioning," weakens your dog's fear, whether of strangers, men in uniforms, noises, or something else, by helping him associate what he's afraid of with something good. The fear may disappear altogether if the approach is used consistently over an extended time period. An excellent handbook on this topic is *The Cautious Canine: How to Help Dogs Conquer Their Fears* by Patricia B. McConnell, PhD.

Barking, a normal canine behavior, becomes a problem behavior when your dog barks excessively.

for barking until you pay attention. When your Poodle can't speak to you in English, he speaks to you in bark.

Poodles are dogs who need companionship and vigorous exercise. When they don't get enough time with you and chances to run, jump, and play, they can become pests, and one surefire way to get attention is barking. Your dog needs your undivided attention several times a day. That means playing together, cuddling, learning a new trick. Maybe even going to an obedience class. Something to say, "Hey pal, you're important to me, and I'm glad you're my dog. Let's have some fun."

The home-alone woofs usually mean your Poodle is bored, uncomfortable, or anxious. Make sure his basic needs for food, potty time, and something to do during the day are met. Before you leave home (having taken him out to potty), ask yourself some questions. Has he had enough exercise? Has he had face time? Is he a little tired? Neighbors probably won't hear much barking, because your dog has what he needs. Have you provided toys to keep him busy? Rotate the toy selection to make older toys seem new and more interesting. Always include one filled with treats or a busy-box toy.

When your Poodle's needs have been met and he's still barking when you're not home, he may have separation anxiety, which means experiencing serious emotional distress when you're gone. Separation anxiety requires more complex training. Consult a professional trainer or behaviorist and conduct further research if your dog shows signs of this condition.

If you're having a tough time personally or professionally and you know your Poodle is not getting what he needs, invest in dog daycare. Daycare can be expensive, but this service is an excellent way to increase your dog's activity level, giving him mental and physical stimulation, while you continue to work through your own struggles. Dogs are social animals. You brought one into your home to provide companionship—and that's a two-way agreement. You have a responsibility to provide companionship and exercise for your dog.

Stop Rewarding Barking

When your Poodle knows the rules, he will follow them, as long as they're consistent and you don't reward him for rule breaking. Unfortunately, rewarding barking is easy because your dog wants your attention most of all. When he barks and you pick him up to calm him down, you've solved the problem today but have contributed to the problem tomorrow, when he barks again. By comforting him when he's barking (or giving him treats to quiet him down, or even yelling which scares him but also gives him your attention, his greatest conquest), you're teaching him that barking gets him good things. You're training him to bark.

How can you untrain him? Give him something better to do. One way to stop your dog from barking when people come to the door is to bring him into another room, tell him to lie down, reward him with a treat for complying, close that door, and answer the other door. Or maybe your spouse can bring him out the back door for a romp in the yard. Distractions like these can help resolve situations without encouraging your dog to bark for rewards.

Put Barking (and Not Barking) on Cue

In a fit of genius, a trainer once suggested putting *speak* and *quiet* on cue. Although this is not the first solution you might have thought of, it is a proven solution. You teach the commands in a neutral situation. Then you use them in a situation that has been a problem. While you eliminate the rewarding of the barking behavior through distraction, you develop a way to stop the barking when it starts. Ask a trainer how to put these behaviors on cue.

Gauging the Problem Behavior

Barking isn't always easy to deal with, especially if your neighbors are as frustrated as you are. While you're working on the issue, tell your neighbors that you know

Ask your trainer to show you how to put the commands *speak* and *quiet* on cue.

what's going on and that you're taking steps to resolve it. They can help you solve the problem by helping you ascertain when your dog barks the most to give you a better idea of the scope of the problem and its possible causes. Other good ways to get an idea of when your dog barks are walking around the block and listening for a while or recording audio or video in your house while you're away at work.

Why Not a Bark Collar?

Bark collars deliver a shock to your dog whenever he barks and should never be used. They are not only inhumane (and punish your dog for barking even when barking might be necessary), but they foster aggression and make the underlying problems that cause excessive barking worse. Citronella collars, which spray an unpleasant scent whenever your dog barks, are not as extreme, but they should only be used as a last resort, after seeing a professional trainer or behaviorist.

CHEWING

Puppies are prone to chewing, often due to teething (and don't underestimate how much energy they have!), but adult dogs also have the chewing instinct. When your Poodle chews chew toys, his chewing is not a problem behavior, but when he chews your shoes or other inappropriate objects, it can be. Luckily, you can solve chewing through prevention, substitution, and consistency.

HOW TO SOLVE CHEWING

Chewing forbidden items needs a response on several levels because a dog's inappropriate selection of items is usually caused by more than one problem. Often your Poodle doesn't have enough around the house to chew, isn't getting enough exercise, and doesn't understand which items are inappropriate to chew.

Prevention

Preventing your Poodle from accessing inappropriate chewing items is an easy way to stop the behavior. Keep your shoes in the closet, keep your bedroom door closed, keep the remotes in a drawer near the television. Consider using baby gates or exercise pens as a temporary solution, but remember that limiting your dog's ability to roam will also bottle up his energy.

It's not always possible to prevent theft. If you discover that your dog has absconded with your new cross-trainers, don't chase him. First, you won't catch him, and second, that's probably what he wants. If possible, grab a tasty treat and call, "Look, Hamilton, a treat!" He may drop the shoe and eat the treat while you retrieve your footwear. You could also plan ahead by asking a trainer about the *drop it* command.

Once you've regained control of your property (the shoe, not the dog), remember to keep it out his reach next time. Then take your Poodle out for a brisk walk to clear your minds. When you come back, provide him with an appropriate chew toy.

Don't leave anything out that you don't want your Poodle to have access to.

Alternative Chewing

Give your Poodle enough to chew on. Chew toys are great for helping satisfy his chewing urges. Make sure you choose the right chew toy for your dog's strength and size (toys that are too soft can quickly be ingested, while those that are too hard or hazardously shaped can hurt your dog's teeth), and get a new one when the old one gets whittled down. Treat balls can be great, both for giving your dog something to chew and giving him an engaging activity.

"What About the Coffee Table?"

If your Poodle is chewing on something that's not easy to hide, there are solutions. You could restrict his access to

certain items with baby gates, exercise pens, and closed doors, keeping in mind that he should not be cooped up all day. You could also spray the object with a nontoxic dog repellent, which may smell or taste unpleasant. If your dog keeps returning to one specific inappropriate object, you may want to replace it. The object may have a smell that attracts your dog.

DIGGING

Digging is a natural part of the prey drive that many dogs have. Although Poodles were not bred to dig, like Dachshunds and some terriers were, there are some who love it. Once a dog gets the notion to dig, there are a few ways to deal with his behavior.

HOW TO SOLVE DIGGING

If your Poodle is digging, you can't leave him in the yard without you. He'll be digging up everything in sight. You might want to create a fenced cement run. Useful under any circumstances, he won't be digging there.

You could also let your Poodle dig where he's not causing trouble. People in rural areas might have patches of land where they can bring their dog on bath day (before the bath!) and encourage him to dig. Another solution is to build a "dig pit" for your Poodle. This is definitely more work, but it can be done. Many families with digging dogs put toys in a sand pit and encourage them to dig there.

JUMPING UP

Does your Poodle jump on your guests to greet them? You'll know if you have this problem if guests or people on the street back away from him. Though this behavior can be considered cute, senior citizens, small children, and people scared of dogs could be seriously hurt. And you're telling your dog that you think this is excellent behavior when you allow it.

If your Standard Poodle starts as a puppy, maybe it's not so bad—but think about when he grows up to be 70 pounds (32 kg). And even the smaller Poodles can seem overwhelming when they are jumping on your niece who's three.

HOW TO SOLVE JUMPING UP

Because jumping up is based on foreseeable circumstances and cooperation, modifying this behavior can be accomplished with consistent practice. When your Poodle starts jumping up, ignore him, standing solidly or blocking the jump with your palms. (Never knee him in the chest or try to shove him away; these actions can seem like a game to your dog, harm him, or promote aggression.) Keep your activity low-key and avoid eye contact until he's calm enough to sit down. Then tell him, "Good," and pet him.

Do this every time your Poodle jumps up and he'll start to lose interest in this activity because it doesn't get the reaction he's hoping for. Ask your guests to follow the program, perhaps inviting friends over for your dog to practice with. With enough people consistently showing no response to your Poodle's jumping up and giving him attention when he's calm, he should get the idea.

Withdrawing your attention when your Poodle jumps up may reduce the behavior.

Guest Training

One good partner-based training process involves using the *sit-stay*. First have your dog become good enough with the command sequence to stay for two minutes. Then have him sit and stay on leash while your training partner opens the front door from the inside. Keep the leash short enough that he cannot reach the door (saying, "No," when he tries to). Only reward him when he stays while the door is opened.

When he consistently succeeds with that, you can put him in a *sit-stay* and have your partner knock on the door from outside, repeating the same process (without the leash, this time) until he stays while you admit your guest. Then reward him. Make sure your guest doesn't acknowledge your dog unless he's successfully completed the *stay*.

On-Leash Training

If your Poodle is in the habit of jumping on you while he is leashed, try standing on the leash while giving him just enough slack so that he can stand comfortably. From here, if he tries to spring into the air, the leash simply won't allow it. When he does try to jump up, say, "No," and turn away. Reward him for quietly standing with all four feet on the floor.

LEASH PULLING

When you walk your Poodle and there is no slack in the leash, your Poodle is pulling. This can hamper both of your afternoons in terms of enjoyment, but it's relatively simple to resolve.

HOW TO SOLVE LEASH PULLING

When your dog starts pulling on the leash, try the "stand still" method. Keep your elbows bent and the leash in a two-handed grip (pinkies next to dog). Every time the leash goes taut from pulling, say "No," and stand like a post until your dog stops pulling and returns to your side. Then praise immediately. You may not get very far in your walks at first, but he'll soon get the idea that he's not going anywhere by pulling on the leash.

NIPPING

Puppies use their mouths to explore the world, so nipping behavior is not unusual for younger dogs. Because nipping hurts people and becomes more serious as your dog grows up, however, this behavior should be resolved as soon as possible.

No matter his size, if your adult Poodle is nipping or

Dog Tale

We've all seen a dog misbehaving. The more the human says, "Bad Spot, don't do that," the more excited the dog becomes, until the behavior has spiraled out of control. If you interrupt the dog's behavior early—say, by walking briskly forward and taking a walk around the block—the dog will be too busy to misbehave.

showing signs of aggression (which include deep growling, baring his teeth and staring, standing tall with his shoulder hair raised and his tail straight up, and biting), get professional help. Aggressive behavior can be directed toward you, your family, other people, or other pets.

HOW TO SOLVE NIPPING

Nipping behavior can be resolved relatively simply through consistent correction. Every time your puppy uses his teeth to pinch your skin, give him a sharp "Oww!" so that he learns that it hurts when he mouths you that way. Then stand up and turn your back on him ("Play nice or not at all"). Withdrawing your attention shows your puppy that nipping doesn't get him what he wants.

WHEN TO SEEK PROFESSIONAL HELP

When problem behaviors are causing your family to be afraid, your neighbors to complain, and you to consider giving your dog away, they have gotten out of hand. While many behaviors can be handled by dog owners themselves, when they continue and you feel unable to manage them yourself, seek professional help.

A certified professional dog trainer (ccpdt.org) or certified applied animal behaviorist (CAAB) (animalbehaviorsociety.org) will guide you on how to realistically correct your dog's behavior. She will also show you what you're saying to your dog through your voice and posture. You may be very surprised at your miscommunication and what your dog's posture says in return. Finally, she will help you understand your Poodle's intentions. Dogs aren't trying to punish you or make your life difficult. Their motivations are more basic, and a professional trainer or behaviorist can help you uncover the causes for their behavior.

Sometimes problems are health related. If you suspect that your dog's problem behaviors have a medical basis, consult a member of the American College of Veterinary Behaviorists (ACVB) (dacvb.org). These veterinarians can help you assess whether your dog's patterns have a health-related cause. In addition, they can recommend trainers or other professionals who may be able to help you once the immediate "crisis" has passed.

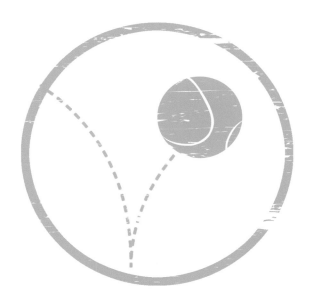

ACTIVITIES WITH YOUR POODLE

Nothing cements a bond between two friends like going bowling together or slogging over the wet countryside in search of pheasants. Poodles may look chic and elegant, but let's face it—they were originally bred for sloshing through marshes after birds and still retain a sporting spirit. Don't worry if none of these activities seems interesting to you, though. There are plenty of other choices. All of them help bind you together, some also help others, and most give you a semi-decent workout.

With so many possible ways to have fun with your Poodle, you'll want to be sure to explore, in this chapter, the activities you and Poodle can do on your own and in the community, from getting the Canine Good Citizen (CGC) certification to playing sports, doing therapy work, and traveling.

SPORTS AND ACTIVITIES

Every dog sport has its own partisans, its own community, and its own panel of experts, most of whom are happy to welcome new members. The Poodle Club of America (PCA) provides information about dog shows, obedience trials, and other formal tests of Poodle prowess on their website: poodleclubofamerica.org.

If you're not interested in shows or competition, don't despair. Poodles will happily, though condescendingly, accompany you while you're camping, jogging,

Agility is a sport made for Poodles' enthusiasm, energy, and brains.

and elsewhere, more to keep you out of trouble than anything else. You seldom go wrong with a Poodle at your side.

AGILITY

Agility is definitely a Poodle-friendly sport. It draws on all his special attributes: speed, brains, energy, and obedience. It also satisfies his need to show off. Agility is one of the fastest-growing sports in the dog world, and with good reason: it's exciting to watch and fun to compete in.

In this sport the handler (you) directs the athlete (Murray, your Poodle) over a series of obstacles: jumps, tunnels, A-frame ramps, teeter–totters, weave poles, fences. The competition is timed: the fastest dog to go clean is the winner. The tricky part is memorizing the course. That's your job.

Agility is truly a team sport, and successful competitors develop a strong and trusting relationship. Poodles of all three sizes can compete equally since the sizes of the obstacles are geared to the height of the dog. Many kennel clubs and other dog fancier groups offer agility classes (some even indoors) for aspiring athletes. It's a good idea to take a few of these since it's harder to retrain your dog than to train him right in the first place. You'll find a mentor at these clubs.

CAMPING

Poodles much prefer five-star hotels to tents, but they are good-natured enough to cater to your more primitive instincts as long as you remember to bring all their stuff, which includes food, water, a first-aid kit, medicines, vet records, leashes, toys, extra towels, and the latest issue of *GQ* or *Cosmo*. Your Poodle trusts that you will take him to a park that actually permits dogs. Some less enlightened owners do not.

CANINE FREESTYLE

Perhaps the most colorful dog sport, canine freestyle involves choreographed dance routines showcasing the relationship and athleticism you share with your dog. So it's dancing with the canine stars. Routines involve proficient use of the heel and front positions (augmented with movements like spinning, weaving, and backing up), but they should transcend the obedience aesthetic, culminating in multifaceted performances built on the progression of the music.

Obedience training is an essential prerequisite for freestyle, which marries academic dedication with joyous celebration. Freestyle participants, both human and canine, love their training and enjoy demonstrating their work to an audience. For more information about canine freestyle, check out the Canine

Freestyle Federation website (canine-freestyle.org) and the World Canine Freestyle Organization (WCFO) website (worldcaninefreestyle.crg).

The Canine Good Citizen (CGC) test measures how well your Poodle behaves in society.

CANINE GOOD CITIZEN® PROGRAM

The American Kennel Club (AKC) Canine Good Citizen (CGC) test is a good indicator of how well your Poodle behaves in human society. The CGC certification s not only sometimes required for canine therapy work and other activities but also comes in handy for showing landlords how well behaved your dog is. Training for this test also forms a helpful foundation for canine sports, which require the same discipline and manners that the CGC program evaluates.

The CGC test has 10 parts, which include challenges like graciously greeting a friendly stranger, walking through a crowd politely, and responding to basic commands. Before your dog takes the test, the AKC requires that you sign the Responsible Dog Owner's Pledge, which states that you will provide good care for your dog, keep him safe, ensure that he shows consideration for your neighborhood and society, and give him a good life.

Any Poodle—young or old—who has received the basic immunizations is eligible. Your Poodle can probably be educated to meet the CGC standards within about six to eight weeks, given one hour of instruction each week and 15 minutes of training and review each day. CGC certification classes can help you prepare for the test within this time frame. For more information about the CGC program and related training in your area, consult the AKC website at akc.org.

CONFORMATION

Conformation is a fancy way of saying "dog show." This is an arena where the showy Poodle, with his sparkling personality and commanding air, really has an advantage. A dog show is a giant elimination contest in which each competing dog is compared to the ideal member of his breed. The dog most closely approximating that elusive ideal, at least in the judge's opinion, is pronounced the winner.

These shows were originally designed for breeders to show off their stock, and so even today, most shows don't allowed spayed or neutered dogs to compete. This is a great disappointment for the average pet owner. However, if you have a "show quality" puppy (as evaluated by his breeder), consider delaying his operation. Conformation may be a road you wish to pursue.

Although it looks easy, there's more to conformation than meets the eye. Not only do you need to learn the fundamentals of exhibiting your dog, but you also have to work on your handling skills. (Competing dogs have to learn to pose, or "stack," too.) Still, many owners like to show their own dogs and do so beautifully. Poodle clubs run workshops to help members learn handling and other show-related skills.

Poodles, of course, have to be groomed and clipped correctly, a job best left to a show groomer or breeder rather than Nancy the Pet Groomer around the corner. Grooming a Poodle for a show is an arcane affair that involves many kinds of scissors and blades, mysterious powders, and the even more mysterious eye of the show groomer, who grooms your Poodle to highlight his strong points and downplay the rest.

To compete in AKC conformation, dogs must be registered with the AKC or an accepted foreign breed registry and be six months of age or older. Miniature and Standard Poodles show as members of the Non-Sporting Group; Toy Poodles show as members of the Toy Group. People seriously interested in conformation are encouraged to plan ahead before adopting their Poodle.

FLYBALL

Flyball is a fast-paced sport for dogs who like to run, jump, and catch tennis balls. Each flyball team has four dogs, and each dog completes the flyball course in sequence. The course features four hurdles set in alignment with a box at the end. When a dog reaches and presses the box, a tennis ball is released into the air. He catches the ball and carries it back over the four hurdles to the starting point, where the next dog starts his run.

Any Poodle variety can compete, as hurdle height is

PUPPY POINTER

Six months old is the usual age to qualify for participating in competition, even though most Poodles are not mature enough at that age to compete.

established based on each team's smallest member. According to the North American Flyball Association's (NAFA) offical rules, the minimum jump height is 7 inches (18 cm), and the maximum height is 14 inches (35.5 cm). Even the tennis balls are matched to the size of the dog.

According to NAFA, flyball began in the late 1960s. Before they had flyball boxes to launch the tennis balls, someone stood at the end of each course and threw them. Official tournaments didn't begin until the 1980s, but NAFA now endorses flyball clubs and tournaments throughout North America. For more information about flyball events, teams, and training, visit the NAFA website (flyball.org).

JOGGING

Poodles like to jog. A quick pace shows off their elegant gait and handsome profile; it's a great opportunity for them to perfect their regal attitude. A suitable leash and your Poodle's harness or collar are all you need, plus some doggie bags. Not the restaurant kind—the kind you need for picking up after Pierre.

Before you take up this hobby, be sure that both of you are in good shape. If you haven't exercised together recently, start slowly. Always stop when your dog shows signs of slowing down, and bring water and a portable bowl to help prevent dehydration and overheating. Running during the day is recommended so that everyone can see you, but if you're running at night, equip your Poodle with a fluorescent safety vest and safety lights. Get some for yourself, too.

OBEDIENCE

Obedience teams compete at various skill levels, the three main classes being Novice, Open, and Utility. The Novice class evaluates basic training skills, with exercises like *recall* (*come*), *heel*, and *stay*. The Open class increases the challenge of the basic commands and brings in advanced exercises like retrieving and jumping. The Utility class increases the challenge further with additions like scent discrimination and commands performed with hand signals only.

Obedience trials showcase well-trained dogs and give owners a chance to further enjoy their companionship. Check out the AKC website (akc.org) for more information about obedience, including listings for obedience clubs offering training classes and events.

Obedience trails showcase well-trained dogs and give their owners a chance to further enjoy their companionship. Check out the AKC website (akc.org) for more information about obedience, including listings for obedience clubs offering training classes and events.

THERAPY WORK

What brightens your day more than seeing your dog? Dogs brighten the days of almost everyone they meet, and one great way to get yours involved in the community is to have him certified as a therapy dog. Therapy dogs visit nursing homes, schools, hospitals, and other places where they can provide people with love and compassion.

Only the most good-natured dogs are accepted, because therapy dog organizations have to make sure that their helpers will show love to everyone they meet (along with being peaceable around other dogs and pets). Consult the Therapy Dogs International website (tdi-dog.org) or another therapy dog organization for more information about the approval process.

TRAVEL

Families often travel together, and when a Poodle is part of your family, that doesn't have to change. When your destination allows dogs, it makes sense to bring your Poodle along for the adventure. Of course, sometimes having him stay home makes more sense. If you're going to Disney World, there's no admission ticket for your Poodle, and for larger dogs, air travel should usually be avoided if possible. Whether you're bringing your dog or keeping him home, you can always make sure he stays safe and happy.

Dog Tale

One longtime Poodle parent had a Standard Poodle who loved the snow, so she decided to try skijoring. A blend of cross-country skiing and mushing, skijoring allows your harnessed Poodle to run through the snow while pulling you on a towline attached to your own harness. With your skis and poles, you do the rest!

Since Poodles aren't built for the cold like Siberian Huskies are, make sure yours is properly outfitted for the snow, and don't stay out too long. And of course, you shouldn't go skijoring with a puppy, who may not be physically developed enough. Check into other safety precautions before taking on this sport. For more information, visit sleddogcentral.com/skijoring.htm.

BY CAR

Travel by car makes it easy to include your Poodle, the tourist of dogs. His crate should always be in the car, ready to go. While driving, keep your dog restrained for his safety and yours. During car accidents (especially at highway speeds, but even at 30 miles per hour [48.5 kmph]), unrestrained dogs are flung forward with immense force. Dogs can also contribute to accidents by distracting the driver.

So restrained dogs make for safer driving, and there are several restraining devices you can choose from. Secured travel crates are commonly considered a good option. Your dog should feel comfortable inside his crate, and as long as it's secured, it shouldn't move during sudden stops. Car seats with security attachments and seat harnesses are also available. Their disadvantage is that dogs can chew through them at the most inopportune times.

Dogs, of course, may want to ride without these restrictions. The best incentive for getting dogs into their restraining devices happily is having already developed positive associations with them. Practice feeding meals or treats while your dog sits in the travel crate, car seat, or seat harness for several days before expecting him to be cooperative about his restraint.

BY PLANE

Traveling with your dog by plane can be dangerous. The best-case scenario is that he is small enough to bring into the cabin with you. Not every airline allows this, but if yours does, request written approval that you can carry him

POODLE

128

on when you book your flight. There may be additonal fees, but having him fly in the cabin is well worth it.

If your dog cannot fly in the cabin, his accommodations won't be nearly as good as yours. Pets checked as cargo travel with the luggage, where excessive heat or cold, insufficient ventilation, or improper handling may cause your pet not to survive the trip. He may also be lost, depending on what happens with the luggage and whether you have connecting flights. Because of the risk, seriously consider driving or leaving your Poodle at home if he cannot fly in the cabin.

DOG-FRIENDLY LODGING

Dog-friendly hotels can be found all over the world. Check out websites like dogfriendly.com to find lodging that accepts pets where you're traveling. There may be a security deposit involved. Before you leave, make sure your Poodle is housetrained and crate trained, behaves well around others, and isn't likely to make a mess or bark through the night.

You should always bring your dog's crate (along with his toys, food, and other supplies), but make sure he won't be cooped up in the hotel room throughout your trip. The fun of bringing him along is that he can enjoy the vacation with you. If your dog would be a burden on your vacation, explore your options for leaving him behind instead.

Keep your Poodle restrained during car travel for his safety and yours.

WHEN YOUR POODLE STAYS BEHIND

When you can't take your Poodle with you, you have choices about how to provide care for him. One popular option is the pet sitter, who cares for your dog in your home. Of course, finding the right sitter is everything. Good pet sitters have experience, references, backup plans, access to emergency veterinary services, and even liability insurance. Some stay with your dog throughout your vacation, while others make daily visits.

With pet sitters, your first concern is your Poodle's well-being. You can find reliable pet sitters through your local Poodle club, your veterinarian (many veterinary technicians offer pet sitting services), or a professional pet sitting organization. Two well-known organizations are Pet Sitters International (PSI) (petsit.com) and the National Association of Professional Pet Sitters (NAPPS) (petsitters.org). Local members are listed on their websites.

Not interested in pet sitters? Consider a boarding facility. You'll want some recommendations and to make a personal visit before leaving your Poodle at a kennel. Again, your first concern is your dog's well-being. Acceptable kennels require health certificates providing evidence that your dog's vaccinations are up to date. Staff should be experienced in handling the emergencies that can

When you leave your Poodle behind, your first concern should be his well-being.

arise in the kennel setting. Many dog daycare services offer boarding, as do some veterinary hospital extensions, so you may know a good place already.

You should consider forming a relationship with a local pet sitter or boarding facility as soon as your Poodle comes home. That way you'll be prepared to give him good care no matter where your adventures take you—even if those adventures leave your Poodle behind.

RESOURCES

ASSOCIATIONS AND ORGANIZATIONS

BREED CLUBS

American Kennel Club (AKC)
8051 Arco Corporate Drive,
Suite 100
Raleigh, NC 27617-3390
Telephone: (919) 233-9767
E-mail: info@akc.org
www.akc.org

Canadian Kennel Club (CKC)
200 Ronson Drive, Suite 400
Etobicoke, Ontario M9W 5Z9
Telephone: (416) 675-5511
Fax: (416) 675-6506
E-mail: information@ckc.ca
www.ckc.ca

Fédération Cynologique Internationale (FCI)
FCI Office
Place Albert 1er, 13
B-6530 Thuin
Belgique
Telephone: +32 71 59.12.38
Fax: +32 71 59.22.29
www.fci.be

The Kennel Club (KC) (UK)
Telephone: 01296 318540
Fax: 020 7518 1058
www.thekennelclub.org.uk

Poodle Club of America (PCA)
E-mail: infopoodleclubofamerica@
yahoo.com
www.poodleclubofamerica.org

Poodle Club of America Rescue Foundation (PCARF)
E-mail: poodleclubofamerica@
yahoo.com
www.poodleclubofamerica
rescuefoundationinc.org

The Standard Poodle Club (UK)
standardpoodleclub.com

United Kennel Club (UKC)
100 E. Kilgore Road
Kalamazoo, MI 49002-5584
Telephone: (269) 343-9020
Fax: (269) 343-7037
www.ukcdogs.com

PET SITTERS

National Association of Professional Pet Sitters (NAPPS)
1120 Route 73, Suite 200
Mount Laurel, New Jersey 08054
Telephone: (856) 439-0324
Fax: (856) 439-0525
E-mail: napps@petsitters.org
www.petsitters.org

Pet Sitters International (PSI)
Telephone: (336) 983-9222
E-mail: info@petsit.com
www.petsit.com

RESCUE ORGANIZATIONS AND ANIMAL WELFARE GROUPS

American Humane Association
1400 16th Street NW, Suite 360
Washington, DC 20036
Telephone: (800) 227-4645
E-mail: info@americanhumane.org
www.americanhumane.org

American Society for the Prevention of Cruelty to Animals (ASPCA)
424 E. 92nd Street
New York, NY 10128-6804
Telephone: (212) 876-7700
www.aspca.org

Royal Society for the Prevention of Cruelty to Animals (RSPCA)
RSPCA Advice Team
Wilberforce Way
Southwater
Horsham
West Sussex
RH13 9RS
United Kingdom
www.rspca.org.uk

SPORTS

International Agility Link (IAL)
85 Blackwall Road
Chuwar, Queensland
Australia 4306
www.lowchensaustralia.com/
shows/international-agility-link.
htm

North American Dog Agility Council (NADAC)
24605 Dodds Road
Bend, Oregon 97701
www.nadac.com

North American Flyball Association (NAFA)
1333 West Devon Avenue, #512
Chicago, IL 60660
Telephone: (800) 318-6312
Fax: (800) 318-6312
E-mail: flyball@flyball.org
www.flyball.org

United States Dog Agility Association (USDAA)
PO Box 850955
Richardson, TX 75085
Telephone: (972) 487-2200
Fax: (972) 231-9700
www.usdaa.com

World Canine Freestyle Organization (WCFO)
4547 Bedford Avenue
Brooklyn, NY 11235
Telephone: (718) 332-8336
E-mail: wcfodogs@aol.com
www.worldcaninefreestyle.org

THERAPY
Alliance of Therapy Dogs (ATD)
PO Box 20227
Cheyenne, WY 82003
Telephone: (877) 843-7364
Fax: (307) 638-2079
E-mail: therapydogsinc@qwestoffice.net
www.therapydogs.com

Pet Partners
875 124th Ave NE, #101
Bellevue, WA 98005
Telephone: (425) 679-5500
www.petpartners.org

Therapy Dogs International (TDI)
88 Bartley Road
Flanders, NJ 07836
Telephone: (973) 252-9800
Fax: (973) 252-7171
E-mail: tdi@gti.net
www.tdi-dog.org

TRAINING
American College of Veterinary Behaviorists (ACVB)
College of Veterinary Medicine, 4474 TAMU
Texas A&M University
College Station, Texas 77843-4474
www.dacvb.org

American Kennel Club Canine Health Foundation (CHF)
PO Box 900061
Raleigh, NC 27675
Telephone: (888) 682-9696
Fax: (919) 334-4011
www.akcchf.org

Animal Behavior Society (ABS)
2111 Chestnut Ave, Suite 145
Glenview, IL 60025
Telephone: (312) 893-6585
Fax: (312) 896-5619
E-mail: info@animalbehaviorsociety.org
www.animalbehaviorsociety.org

Association of Professional Dog Trainers (APDT)
2365 Harrodsburg Road A325
Lexington, KY 40504
Telephone: (800) 738-3647
Fax: (864) 331-0767
www.apdt.com

Certification Council for Professional Dog Trainers (CCPDT)
Professional Testing Corporation
1350 Broadway, 17th Floor
New York, NY 10018
Telephone: (855) 362-3784
E-mail: administrator@ccpdt.org
www.ccpdt.org

International Association of Animal Behavior Consultants (IAABC)
565 Callery Road
Cranberry Township, PA 16066
www.iaabc.org

National Association of Dog Obedience Instructors (NADOI)
7910 Picador Drive
Houston, TX 77083-4918
Telephone: (972) 296-1196
E-mail: info@nadoi.org
www.nadoi.org

VETERINARY AND HEALTH RESOURCES

Academy of Veterinary Homeopathy (AVH)
PO Box 232282
Leucadia, CA 92023-2282
Telephone: (866) 652-1590
Fax: (866) 652-1590
theavh.org

American Academy of Veterinary Acupuncture (AAVA)
PO Box 803
Fayetteville, TN 37334
Telephone: (931) 438-0238
Fax: (931) 433-6289
www.aava.org

American Animal Hospital Association (AAHA)
12575 W. Bayaud Ave
Lakewood, CO 80228-2021
Telephone: (303) 986-2800
Fax: (303) 986-1700
E-mail: info@aaha.org
www.aaha.org

American College of Veterinary Internal Medicine (ACVIM)
1997 Wadsworth Boulevard
Lakewood, CO 80214-5293
Telephone: (303) 231-9933
Telephone (US or Canada): (800) 245-9081
Fax: (303) 231-0880
E-mail: ACVIM@ACVIM.org
www.acvim.org

American College of Veterinary Ophthalmologists (ACVO)
PO Box 1311
Meridian, ID 83680
Telephone: (208) 466-7624
Fax: (208) 466-7693
E-mail: office15@acvo.org
www.acvo.org

American Heartworm Society (AHS)
PO Box 8266
Wilmington, DE 19803-8266
E-mail: info@heartwormsociety.org
www.heartwormsociety.org

American Holistic Veterinary Medical Association (AHVMA)
33 Kensington Parkway
Abingdon, MD 21009
Telephone: (410) 569-0795
Fax: (410) 569-2346
E-mail: office@ahvma.org
www.ahvma.org

American Veterinary Medical Association (AVMA)
1931 North Meacham Road, Suite 100
Schaumburg, IL 60173-4360
Telephone: (800) 248-2862
Fax: (847) 925-1329
www.avma.org

ASPCA Animal Poison Control
Telephone: (888) 426-4435
www.aspca.org/pet-care/animal-poison-control

British Veterinary Association (BVA)
7 Mansfield Street
London
W1G 9NQ
United Kingdom
Telephone: 020 7636 6541
Fax: 020 7908 6349
E-mail: bvahq@bva.co.uk
www.bva.co.uk

Orthopedic Foundation for Animals (OFA)
2300 E. Nifong Boulevard
Columbia, MO 65201-3806
Telephone: (573) 442-0418
Fax: (573) 875-5073
E-mail: ofa@offa.org
www.offa.org

US Food and Drug Administration Center for Veterinary Medicine (CVM)
US Food and Drug Administration
Communications Staff (HFV-12)
7519 Standish Place
Rockville, MD 20855
Telephone: (240) 402-7002
E-mail: AskCVM@fda.hhs.gov
www.fda.gov/AnimalVeterinary/

PUBLICATIONS
BOOKS
Adamson, Eve, with Sandy Roth. *Complete Guide to Dog Grooming: Skills, Techniques, and Instructions for the Home Groomer.* Animal Planet. Neptune City: TFH Publications, Inc., 2011.

Biniok, Janice. *The Toy & Miniature Poodle.* Terra-Nova. With consulting veterinary editor Wayne Hunthausen, DVM. Neptune City: TFH Publications, Inc., 2006.

Fernandez, Amy. *Poodles.* Animal Planet Pet Care Library. Neptune City: TFH Publications, Inc., 2008.

King, Trish. *Parenting Your Dog: Develop Dog-Rearing Skills for a Well-Trained Companion.* Neptune City: TFH Publications, Inc., 2010.

Wood, Deborah. *Little Dogs: Training Your Pint-Sized Companion.* TFH Publications, Inc., 2004.

MAGAZINES
AKC Family Dog
American Kennel Club
260 Madison Avenue
New York, NY 10016
www.akc.org/pubs/family-dog/

AKC Gazette
American Kennel Club
260 Madison Avenue
New York, NY 10016
www.akc.org/pubs/gazette/

WEBSITES
Nylabone
www.nylabone.com

TFH Publications, Inc.
www.tfh.com

INDEX

ABOUT THE AUTHORS

Writer and educator **Carol Frischmann** has been fascinated by pets, nature, and science since she was saved in a childhood accident by the family dog. After earning a BS in Science Education at Duke University, she pursued her love of animals by educating visitors at zoos and museums and by writing books and for magazines, newspapers, and pet columns. Carol teaches at the Grand Canyon School and lives inside the national park.

Diane Morgan has written numerous books on canine care and nutrition and has worked in dog rescue for many years. She is a five-time winner of the Dog Writers Association of America (DWAA) Maxwell Award for excellence in dog writing. Diane also teaches English and philosophy, has worked with indigo snakes, invasive pythons, and pilot whales, and is currently involved in manatee research, advocacy, and rescue. She lives in Vero Beach, Florida.

PHOTO CREDITS

ABOUT ANIMAL PLANET™

Animal Planet™ is the only television network dedicated exclusively to the connection between humans and animals. The network brings people of all ages together by tapping into our fundamental fascination with animals through an array of fresh programming that includes humor, competition, drama, and spectacle from the animal kingdom.

ABOUT *DOGS 101*

The most comprehensive—and most endearing—dog encyclopedia on television, *DOGS 101* spotlights the adorable, the feisty and the unexpected. A wide-ranging rundown of everyone's favorite dog breeds—from the Dalmatian to Xoloitzcuintli —this series surveys a variety of breeds for their behavioral quirks, genetic history, most famous examples and wildest trivia. Learn which dogs are best for urban living and which would be the best fit for your family. Using a mix of animal experts, pop-culture footage and stylized dog photography, *DOGS 101* is an unprecedented look at man's best friend.

At Animal Planet,
we're committed to providing
quality products designed to
help your pets live long,
healthy, and happy lives.